Al Pacino

Anatomy of an Actor

Al Pacino

Karina Longworth

Introduction

"But isn't what I do also who I am? I mean, my work is very consuming; who I am is my work, too."[1]
—Al Pacino, 1979

Crashing Through the Glass Ceiling

He's short—five foot seven, maybe—slight enough in stature that Francis Ford Coppola, the director of *The Godfather*, would make the actor wear lifts in his shoes that made him walk like Donald Duck.[2] He's dark and handsome, but not in the All-American Boy fashion; with his olive skin, bushy eyebrows, and full lips, he's visibly Italian. He trained on the New York stage, and also on the New York streets, observing real people to develop a technique so sly that, at first, it didn't look like "acting" at all. His work may be both what Al Pacino does and who he is, but it took a special confluence of events to make him a movie star.

A decade or two earlier, the movies would not have been ready for him. As an art center and as an industry, Hollywood experienced cataclysmic changes between the late 1960s and the early 1980s. *Bonnie and Clyde* (1967), *The Graduate* (1967), *Easy Rider* (1969)—these films were as different from one another as they were from the Classical Hollywood status quo. But their combined success, coming at a time when the studio system had lost touch with its audience, helped to usher in new business practices, new standards of quality, and, maybe most importantly, an overall openness to new ways of thinking.

Studios begrudgingly began to finance different types of movies for emerging young writers and directors, who in turn propped the door open for a new brand of movie star. The first actor to walk through that door was Dustin Hoffman, cast as *Graduate* protagonist Benjamin Braddock over much likelier suspects such as Warren Beatty and Robert Redford. No one was more surprised than Hoffman himself. "This is not the part for me," he thought. "I'm not supposed to be in movies. I'm supposed to be where I belong—an ethnic actor is supposed to be in ethnic New York, in an ethnic Off-Broadway show! I know my place."[3] Then *The Graduate*, released December 1967, became the highest-grossing film of 1968.

As the film's cowriter Buck Henry put it, Hoffman's success as a romantic hero "brought a sort of social and visual change,"[4] which helped prime American audiences for a new wave of leading men.

A contemporary of Hoffman's in the 1960s New York theater scene, Al Pacino was perhaps the key beneficiary of Hoffman's ascension through the "ethnic" actor glass ceiling. Half a decade after *The Graduate*, 32-year-old Pacino won the role of Michael Corleone in *The Godfather*—a part initially offered to a host of "all-American" stars. The casting would change his life—and, arguably, the literal face of American cinema.

How can we measure Pacino's impact on acting? There is no shortage of breathless assessments of how, with his startling charisma and near-invisible technique, his image "represented a new kind of movie star who was more hoodlum, less Hollywood"[5]; how he "redefined machismo, favoring understated intensity and scruffy grace over brawn... [John Wayne] and his crowd may have personified what men wanted to be, but Pacino—vulnerable and dissatisfied and still somehow winning—showed us what we really were."[6]

But Pacino's success went beyond making Hollywood films safe for a scruffy hoodlum from ethnic New York. The actor arrived on American screens marked as an outsider by his genes and upbringing, but thanks to a series of savvily chosen roles in socially conscious films that appealed to critics and audiences alike (most notably *Serpico* [1973] and *Dog Day Afternoon* [1975], both directed by Sidney Lumet and developed around Pacino's talents), Pacino turned the outsider into the everyman, embodying the troubled masculinity of a culture struggling to cope with changing attitudes toward sex, class, race, and gender, while still under the shadows of Vietnam and Watergate. By the mid-1970s, Al Pacino no longer represented an exception to Hollywood's male ideal—he *was* the ideal.

A Star Is Born

Alfredo James Pacino, the only child of Salvatore and Rose Pacino, was born in 1940. When he was two his parents divorced, and his mom moved

Al Pacino and Hal Holbrook in Don Peterson's 1969 play *Does a Tiger Wear a Necktie?*

Opposite: Charlie Laughton and Al Pacino at the Scandia Restaurant in New York City after a performance of Eugene O'Neill's *A Moon for the Misbegotten*, January 2, 1974.

him from East Harlem to her parents' tiny apartment in the South Bronx, a working-class neighborhood so racially and ethnically mixed that the actor would later describe himself as "a true descendant of the melting pot." Pacino rarely saw his father, but his grandparents hosted a revolving cast of family members. "At one point," Pacino recalled, "there were nine of us living in three rooms."[7]

A rough life was waiting for him on the Bronx streets if he wanted it, and, indeed, two of Pacino's closest friends growing up would die prematurely from drug overdoses. In his youth Pacino was known to act up at school, but his family kept him out of real trouble. He spent a lot of time at home with his grandfather, a first-generation immigrant from, of all places, the small Sicilian town of Corleone. "I guess he knew I was an actor, because I used to love to hear him tell me stories about what it was like in New York in East Harlem in the early 1900s," Pacino recollected in 1979. "He would just string these yarns for hours on the roof."[8]

Pacino was three when his mother started bringing him to the movies. "It was her way of getting out, and she would take me with her," he remembered later. "I'd go home and act all the parts. It had a tremendous influence on my becoming an actor."[9] James Dean was Pacino's early idol. "My mother loved him; I loved him. He had that sense of passing through.

Rebel Without a Cause [Nicholas Ray, 1955] had a very powerful effect on me."[10]

Pacino related to Dean's trademark alienation. He didn't socialize with other kids until starting school at the age of six, and he was shy around people his own age. But he soon learned that he could earn the favor of his peers by making them laugh—pulling pranks on the teacher, showing off on the playground. "If I made a catch at third base," said baseball-loving Pacino, "I'd do a double somersault and sprawl out on the ground." He was also a ham at home, imitating Al Jolson or aping Ray Milland's alcoholic panic from *The Lost Weekend*. But as a little boy, he didn't think of this playacting as the first steps toward his future career. "I wanted to be a baseball player, naturally," he continued. "But I wasn't good enough. I didn't know what I was going to do with my life."[11] When Pacino was fourteen, a drama teacher at school wrote his mother a letter suggesting she encourage his natural talent for performing. That same year he saw a traveling theater troupe perform Chekhov's *The Seagull*. "They probably weren't any good," he said in retrospect, "but I had never seen anything like it in my life. My life was changed that day."[12]

Pacino enrolled in New York's High School of Performing Arts. "That was the only school that would accept me," he admitted. "My scholastic level was not very high." In his acting classes, they taught the "Method" of Russian realist-acting

pioneer Constantin Stanislavski—which bored teenage Pacino to tears. "Once I was in class and had to act out what it was like when I was in my room alone. Since I never had a room to myself, I had to make it up," Pacino said. "I remember how 'natural' the teacher had said I acted. And I went around all the time trying to be natural. I didn't know the difference between being natural and being real. What do I know from Stanislavski? He's Russian, I'm from the Bronx."[13]

When Pacino was sixteen, he dropped out of high school. His mom was sick and needed him to be the breadwinner. Up to this point, she had been an ardent supporter of her son's acting dreams, but now she advised him to be more practical, saying, "Acting is for rich people."[14] Frustrated by his mother's sudden change of heart, Pacino moved out of his grandparents' house and in with a girlfriend. He took on a series of odd jobs and sent money home, but his relationship with his mom remained strained.

After landing a job in the offices of *Commentary* magazine, Pacino began to save money for acting school. He first auditioned for Lee Strasberg's Actors Studio, but was rejected. Instead, he enrolled in classes at Herbert Berghof and Uta Hagen's HB Studio. There he would form a close relationship with Charlie Laughton (not to be confused with Charles Laughton of *Mutiny on the Bounty* fame), who funneled his understanding of acting into teaching, preferring to bring home a steady paycheck to support his daughter and actress wife, Penny Allen—who would later appear opposite Pacino in *Scarecrow* and *Dog Day Afternoon*—over the uncertain life of a performer. Laughton was a decade Pacino's senior, and their meeting, when Pacino was eighteen, marked the beginning of the treasured mentor-protégé relationship to come. "I just felt connected to him," Pacino recollected. "Charlie introduced me to other worlds, to certain aspects of life I wouldn't have come in contact with. He introduced me to writers, the stuff that surrounds acting."[15]

An Off-Off-Broadway production of Strindberg's *The Creditors*, which Pacino starred in under Laughton's direction, was particularly transformative. "For the first time, I knew I had something going for me, a chance to use myself, my life. Charlie Laughton is probably the most important person in my life. He made me realize that acting is poetry, an art that employs the voice, the body, the spirit."[16] With Laughton by his side, Pacino began to file away real life as fodder for future performances. "With no money to go to the theater we'd sit in cafeterias for hours on end, watching the comedies and high dramas taking place," Laughton recalled. "Al got some of his most interesting characters from watching people in the subway and streets of New York."[17]

Then, in 1962, when Pacino was twenty-two, his mother died before the two could fully reconcile. He spent the following few years in extreme poverty and near-suicidal depression. "I was homeless. I slept on the stage of where I was performing. It wasn't fun."[18] He took micro-loans from friends in order to cover basic expenses, spent his nights drinking hard, and for a few years made only a modicum of progress toward the acting career he was by now obsessively pursuing. He tried his hand at stand-up comedy for a while. He moved into a one-room apartment with another struggling actor, Martin Sheen, and together the two wannabes would hang around New York's Living Theatre, taking odd stagehand jobs until Off-Broadway roles began to materialize.

In 1966, Pacino once again auditioned for the Actors Studio. This time, he got in. Paralyzed with fear, it took him six months before he could bring himself to do a monologue in front of the class. When he finally did, Pacino immediately attracted the attention of Actors Studio artistic director Lee Strasberg. Just as Laughton had become a kind of surrogate older brother and acting mentor, Strasberg evolved from Pacino's teacher to his friend and confidant.

Now living with his girlfriend, actress Jill Clayburgh, Pacino was still drinking heavily. He was plagued with guilt over his foolish estrangement from his mother during the last years of her life. But he managed to get cast in an Off-Broadway play, *The Indian Wants the Bronx*, which attracted the attention of Martin Bregman, an entertainment manager who offered Pacino his services. "The play must have cost a buck and a half to put on," Bregman related. "There was just a bare stage, but there was Al. If you think he's terrific on film, you should see him on stage. I knew he'd be a star."[19]

After Pacino won an Obie Award in 1968 for his work in *Bronx*, Bregman helped the tentative actor look for movie work. The idea was that success on the screen could help subsidize his real passion, the stage. Following a bit part in a 1969 Patty Duke vehicle, *Me, Natalie*, Pacino was cast as the heroin-addict lead in *The Panic in Needle Park*, a gritty drama scripted by Joan Didion and John Gregory Dunne, and directed by Jerry Schatzberg. "I turned down eleven movies before I made my first one. I knew it was time for me to get in movies. I didn't know what it would be. When *Panic in Needle Park* came along, Marty Bregman pushed and helped get it together. Without him I don't know what I would have done."[20]

The film was initially banned in Britain, and wasn't released there until 1975—by which time Pacino had become a major star. Considering his first leading role with the benefit of hindsight, the *Sunday Times* of London was able to put the previous half decade into context. "Al Pacino,"

wrote Dilys Powell, had "taken over as the [interpreter] of an uncomfortable world from Brando and Newman. It is Pacino's astonishing ease which strikes one, the fluidity of his movements, the absolute freedom, or so it seems, from the conventions of acting. He doesn't look as if he's giving a performance. *It looks real.*"[21]

The Pacino Essence

Rising to prominence during a period in American cinema in which ambiguity was acceptable like never before (or since), Pacino created indelible characters that were at once street savvy and cerebral, sensitive and vicious, superego and id. As Michael Corleone, he was a savage killer and shrewd businessman, who showed power without saying a word, his only weakness his love for family. As Frank Serpico, he credibly moved between the police academy and the ballet. Pacino's specialty became men with divided natures — cops and lawyers with an allergy to power, criminals whose deeply held belief systems edged them toward heroism. He was a character actor, embodying a range of men from the inside out, while also maintaining enough physical appeal to make him one of the definitive sex symbols of his time. Like the man himself, the quintessential Pacino character contains multitudes, uniting seemingly contradictory elements in a single conflicted soul.

If there is one trademark to Pacino's acting style, one defining element that is present in some way, shape, or form in every screen performance, it is the crescendo and its comedown — an internal, emotional rise and fall that the actor conveys to the audience through body language and vocal cadences. In his first few screen performances, Pacino's exploration of emotional range hews to the character's narrative arc. In *The Godfather*, for instance, Michael's expressiveness decreases steadily, with Pacino gradually working all signs of feeling inward until Michael becomes a completely closed book. In *Scarecrow*, his performance builds over the course of the film from realistic minimalism to an explosion of manic rage. In both cases, when the character is in control, Pacino's technique is almost invisible; the less control the character has over a situation, the more Pacino does and shows.

As Pacino became a bigger star, increasingly playing roles he helped to develop in films produced specifically for him, his crescendo technique, particularly in terms of vocal mechanics, became a way for the actor to assert himself as a presence almost larger than the film itself. Like, say, a saxophonist in a band sneaking in an improvised riff that seems to float above the rest of the ensemble, Pacino has often made his mark through embellishment. The crescendos themselves, instead of building

or falling throughout an entire film, would rise over the course of a single scene (think of the many instances in *Serpico* in which Pacino's undercover cop loses his cool during an exchange) or even a single line of dialogue. Many of Pacino's most famous catchphrases were imprinted into the collective consciousness via his crescendo technique. Think of "Say hello to my little friend!" from *Scarface*: Pacino's reading is more like "Say 'ello to my lil' fren'" Each word is a syncopated note, his volume and intensity rising throughout the measure. Pacino has often spoken of music as an influence, and as a model to aspire to. "I always fantasized myself being in a jazz combo or in the midst of a Beethoven quartet. Just the feeling of getting so far into something," he admitted in 1979. "It hasn't happened in acting, that feeling."[22] Not yet, perhaps, but the musicality he reached for would become increasingly explicit his performances of the 1980s, 1990s, and beyond.

Ten Quintessential Performances

If judged solely by the objective, empirical evidence of box-office popularity, critical reception, and industry accolades, then the ten performances profiled in this book may not be Pacino's ten best. Instead, they are the ten films that I feel most directly evince the Al Pacino essence, and in combination offer a narrative path through the evolution of his talent, his technique, and his persona across his entire career.

Chapter 1 is devoted to Pacino's performance as Michael Corleone in the two-decade-spanning *Godfather Trilogy*. It's a role that can be thought of as a kind of microcosm of the first twenty years of the actor's screen career. Michael arrives in *The Godfather* an unknown youngster, comes back in *The Godfather Part II* a newly crowned king, and returns in *The Godfather Part III* an old-timer with mistakes behind him and redemption on his mind — a path that, in some ways, mirrors Pacino's own evolution from Hollywood newcomer to star to middle-aged veteran looking to recapture past glories. Chapter 2 is devoted to Pacino's performance as a hitchhiker in *Scarecrow*. Filmed between the first two *Godfather* films, Pacino's second collaboration with director Jerry Schatzberg is a film about performance, an examination of natural and unnatural "acting" in social interaction, and an experiment in the possibilities of screen acting to convey private feeling.

Chapters 3 and 4 examine two star vehicles built around Pacino's talents, in collaboration with producer Marty Bregman and director Sidney Lumet, suggesting Pacino's emerging role as the auteur of his own career. *Serpico* gave Pacino his first opportunity to play a living person, and the time he spent with Frank Serpico was revelatory for him. Pacino also played a real person in *Dog Day Afternoon*, although this time he declined to meet the bisexual bank robber his character was based on, preferring to draw on his own experience to fuel improvisations. *Serpico* and *Dog Day Afternoon*, taken together with the film profiled in Chapter 5, Norman Jewison's *...And Justice for All*, form an unofficial trilogy in which Pacino represents essentially good men driven to the edge by the irrational world around them. In other words, he was the voice of the American male of the 1970s.

Chapter 6 examines *Scarface*, a remake of the Howard Hawks gangster classic that Pacino initiated, with Bregman again producing. His performance was completely unlike anything he had done previously (including the requirement that he adopt the accent of a native Spanish speaker), and it would point to his oversize performance style in later films like *Dick Tracy* (1990) and *Devil's Advocate* (1997), opening up the question of what it means to be "over the top," to overreach as a technique and as a philosophy. *Scarface* has become one of Pacino's most popular and frequently quoted films, but it was not appreciated on its initial release. In the mid-1980s, Pacino, disillusioned with Hollywood, retreated into his first love, the theater. In 1989, in need of cash, he returned to the screen to star in *Sea of Love* (Chapter 7). Harold Becker's modern noir marks a key transition in Pacino's career, recasting his star persona from the idealist forced to face defeat to the jaded veteran who is instilled with new faith by his experiences over the course of the film. This transition is emblematic of a fundamental shift in Hollywood, from the brief revolutionary period of the 1970s in which Pacino became a star to the corporate-minded, blockbuster-fueled Hollywood of the late 1980s and 1990s. The film was a hit, but Pacino's comeback was truly cemented with *Scent of a Woman* (Chapter 8), for which he finally won an Oscar.

The second half of Pacino's 40-plus-year film career has had its ups and downs. There have been startling performances, such as his turn as a conflicted detective in Michael Mann's *Heat* (Chapter 9)—the first film in which Pacino shared a scene with his longtime friend, fellow veteran of 1970s New Hollywood, and mirror-image Method actor, Robert De Niro. But in recent years, while racking up less-than-esteemed credits as often as working with serious directors such as Christopher Nolan (*Insomnia*) and Steven Soderbergh (*Ocean's Thirteen*), Pacino has been accused of acting on autopilot for a paycheck, or worse, drifting into self-parody. As if in an attempt to answer these criticisms by showing his detractors what a self-parodic paycheck gig *really* looks like, in 2011 Pacino took the role of "Al Pacino" opposite Adam Sandler in the lowbrow farce *Jack and Jill*

(Chapter 10). Pacino explained he was drawn to playing "himself" as "a guy who just wants to go back home, wants to be simple again, but will never be able to be that way again."[23] A crude, tacky family comedy, *Jack and Jill* is neither high art nor great entertainment, but it offers an unparalleled opportunity to consider the whole of Pacino's career as an actor and as a star, and the transformative impact of his journey from simple beginnings to the pinnacle of his industry had on his acting process. The film also allowed Pacino to come full circle, returning to his first performative pleasure of making people laugh—with him, and at him.

1

Michael Corleone

The Godfather Trilogy (1972, 1974, 1990)
Francis Ford Coppola

"You know, Michael, now that you're so
respectable, I think you're more dangerous than
you ever were. In fact, I preferred you when
you were just a common Mafia hood."
—Kay Adams Michelson, formerly Kay Corleone

With Michael Corleone, the central figure in
Francis Ford Coppola's *Godfather Trilogy*, Al
Pacino was given the role of a lifetime—a vehicle
through which a New York theater actor all but
unknown to movie audiences could make an
indelible entrance into mass culture. Across three
films made over the course of nearly twenty years,
the character goes through a grand evolution:
an empathetic outsider skeptically enters into
a corrupt system, becomes so absorbed by that
system that he trades his selfhood for success
within it, and ages into a wizened survivor
desperately seeking redemption late in life.

Michael's arc loosely resembles the real-life
experience of the actor who played him.
An Italian-American raised penniless by his
immigrant grandparents in the South Bronx
who crossed over from the New York stage
to Hollywood screen stardom, Al Pacino was
transformed through his success. Initially
a symbol of an alternative to the Hollywood
mainstream, he became a primary face of
that mainstream. By the early 1990s, when
The Godfather Part III was made and released,
Pacino was, like his character, visibly worn
down by decades' worth of work and struggle.
The difference is that Michael's attempts at
redemption would end in personal, political,
and commercial defeat, while Pacino, recently
returned to the screen after a few years in the
woods, was on the verge of some of his greatest
achievements, in terms of box-office success
and critical accolades.

But for Pacino, and for Michael, the American
dream of respectability was hard-won, and not
without compromise. Since he plays the same
character at three distinct points in his life, *The
Godfather Trilogy* allows us to watch Pacino at
three distinct points in his career: finding himself
as a screen actor in *The Godfather*, performing
at the peak of his powers and stardom in *The
Godfather Part II*, and attempting to recapture his
former glory in *The Godfather Part III*. The trilogy
acts as a kind of crucible for the actor's evolving

technique, in particular the crescendo effect
that, as we'll see, becomes a crucial part of Pacino's
exploration of a man's emotional response to
power, or lack thereof. In later films, the crescendo
would become a hallmark of Pacino's approach
to a character's expression of emotion over the
course of an act, a scene, or even a single line
reading. But in *The Godfather Trilogy*, Pacino
stretches first emotional withdrawal, and then
an explosion of that repressed feeling, over three
films, spanning two decades. In *The Godfather*,
Michael transforms from college boy to steely
Mafia don, and Pacino gives what critic David
Ansen astutely described as "arguably cinema's
greatest portrait ever of the hardening of a
heart."[24] In *Part II*, Michael's heart remains hard,
but at key moments, as Michael's power slips,
so does his control over his emotions. In *Part III*,
Michael, exhausted by a life of deception and
sorry for his sins, begins to lose the ability to
hide his feelings. As the aged Michael relinquishes
power simultaneous to and as a consequence
of softening his heart, Pacino's performance
becomes bigger, more external, increasingly
operatic. The crescendo hits its peak beautifully
and agonizingly on the steps of an Italian
opera house, with Michael reacting to the death
of his daughter by losing control of his body
and his voice, falling to his knees and emitting
a silent scream.

Coming In from Outside

Each film in *The Godfather Trilogy* begins its
present-day action with a long party scene. In the
first film, it's the wedding of Connie Corleone
(Talia Shire, Coppola's sister), daughter of Don
Vito Corleone (Marlon Brando) and sister to
Fredo (John Cazale), Sonny (James Caan), and
Michael (Pacino). As would become a template
for the series, it's at the party that most of the
film's key players are revealed, their place in this
world indicated by their social interactions with
one another, and with the head of the family.
In *The Godfather*, while guests celebrate Connie's
nuptials in the garden, all manner of business
associates flow in and out of the Don's study—
because, according to Sicilian tradition,
a father cannot refuse a requested favor on
his daughter's wedding day.

Al Pacino as Michael Corleone
in Francis Ford Coppola's *The
Godfather* (1972).

While these meetings give us a sense of what the family business is, the party scene tells us just how far removed Vito's youngest son is from that business. Michael shows up to the wedding late, in his army uniform, with his WASP college girlfriend, Kay, in tow. In Pacino's first dialogue scene as Michael Corleone, he demonstrates the character's gift for diplomacy, using the fewest words possible to get his point across. And here Pacino initiates the audience into his understated approach to the role: as frugal as Michael is with his use of words, Pacino is even more conservative in showing emotion.

When Kay innocently asks why Michael's "brother" Tom Hagen (Robert Duvall) has a different last name, Michael explains that his natural brother Sonny found Tom, an orphan, in the street and the Corleone family took him in. It's a story that makes the family look good. Michael punctuates the anecdote by smilingly asking his girlfriend, "You like your lasagna?" Meaning "Do you like what I'm feeding you?"

After providing a glimpse of the action in Vito's office, Coppola later cuts to the disruptive entrance of Johnny Fontane, the Sinatra-esque crooner who has graced the wedding with an appearance. The still-naïve Kay asks Michael how his family knows this star. Michael matter-of-factly launches into the story of how his father once helped Johnny by making the bandleader who controlled his contract "an offer he couldn't refuse... Luca Brasi held a gun to his head, and my father assured him that either his brains, or his signature, would be on the contract."

Kay is rightly horrified—by the story, and by the way Michael tells it, without emotion, as if it's the most normal family anecdote in the world. Michael quickly calms (and misleads) Kay by shaking his head and saying, "That's my family, Kay. That's not me." But the viewer isn't placated so easily: we know that if she "likes her lasagna," she's going to have to take all that comes with it. The scene swiftly establishes that Michael is, in word and presence, an outsider to the Corleone business, but the narrative of the film will bring him to first tentatively accept, then fully embrace, and finally embody that business.

An Authentic Alternative

Pacino's perceived authenticity—partially due to his physical appearance, and partially to his acting technique—would be the biggest factor in propelling him to stardom. And yet both his identifiable ethnicity and his performance style worked against him in the audition process leading up to *The Godfather*. "He didn't look like a star looked at the time in the business," *Godfather* casting director Fred Roos remembered years later.[25] And so an actor whose grandfather hailed from Corleone, Sicily, was only considered for the role of first-generation Sicilian-American

Michael Corleone after white-bread Hollywood dreamboats Robert Redford and Warren Beatty passed on the part.

Director Francis Ford Coppola felt that Pacino's early, intense performances on the stage and in *The Panic in Needle Park* made the case that he was right for the role of Michael, the college-educated World War II veteran who seeks a life outside the Mafia but is drawn into the family business after an assassination attempt on his father, Don Vito Corleone (Marlon Brando). Coppola swore that a screen test would prove him right. "[A]ll I could see was Al Pacino's face in that camera," Coppola said. "I couldn't get him out of my head. Even when I read the book, I kept seeing him as Michael."[26]

But Pacino was unhappy with the material chosen for his screen test: the opening scene, in which Michael introduces his girlfriend, Kay (Diane Keaton), to his family for the first time. The scene presents Michael at his most subdued and apparently innocent—an important pole to establish in order for his character progression to have meaning. Unsure how to play it, Pacino didn't prepare, and the screen test was a disaster. "[Coppola] took the dullest scene that Michael had, the first wedding scene, which is an exposition scene, and I did it, and he wanted me to do more," Pacino recalled. "I didn't know what he expected me to do."[27] Pacino had to audition three times for the role of Michael. The actor's biggest roadblock was Paramount boy-wonder executive Robert Evans, who swore "that midget" would not land the role. Brando himself placed a call to Evans to try to change his mind. "Pacino, he's a brooder," Brando mumbled. "He's my son." Evans responded, "I'm looking for an actor, not a brooder." But the call convinced Evans to make a deal with Coppola: Pacino was in, as long as James Caan—one of many who had tested for the part of Michael—was cast as Michael's brother Sonny.[28]

Crafting an Enigma

In preparation to play Michael, Pacino conducted clandestine meetings with real-life Mafia players, but he ultimately wouldn't model his performance on these sources. Pacino wanted Michael to be largely inscrutable, not only to other characters but to audiences as well. Mimicry of gestures or body language wasn't going to cut it in order to get the surface effect he wanted; he felt he would have to internalize what Michael was going through. "The thing I was after was to create some kind of enigma, an enigmatic-type person," he said. "So you felt that we were looking at that person and didn't quite know him. When you see Michael in some of those scenes looking wrapped up in a kind of trance, as if his mind was completely filled with thoughts, that's what I was doing. I was actually listening to Stravinsky on the set, so I'd have that look."[29]

18

For Pacino, who had only one leading film role under his belt, *The Godfather* provided an education in finding himself as a movie actor, learning how to make a character progress from scene to scene, even while shooting many takes, and creating the narrative out of order. "The thing that was most difficult about it was doing, say, a scene from the middle of the film during the first week of shooting. I had to think about where I was at that point. I tried to gear myself. I gave it three stages. The first stage was ambivalence. The second was having to cope with what I did—the killings in the restaurant. And then the third was having made the decision of this is the way I'm gonna be. So I broke it up, and I tried to work within that framework."[30] Pacino described the experience as "hellish." "I used to get up at five in the morning thinking about where I was in the film," he explained.[31]

Watching the dailies, Paramount didn't understand what Pacino was going for— they weren't prepared for an actor making the conscious choice to give a performance that was inscrutable. But Pacino was adamant that "Michael has to start out ambivalent, almost unsure of himself and his place. He's caught between his Old World family and the postwar American dream."[32] Given both Michael's uncertainty and his sense of detachment, it helped that Pacino felt like an outsider on set. Despite his alliances with Brando, Coppola, Keaton (whom Pacino would date on and off for two decades), and John Cazale (a frequent stage and screen collaborator of Pacino's), the audition process, and the continued skepticism on the part of Paramount, had made him feel unwanted. His anxiety showed on screen in *The Godfather*'s early scenes—and it made Michael's painful transition from romantic war hero/mob outsider to hardened Mafia don all the stronger.

The film is constructed to give Pacino key scenes at each point in that progression, which gives us our first glimpse of a patented Pacino crescendo. Michael is out Christmas shopping with Kay—all carefree smiles, obliviously in love—when he sees a front-page newspaper headline announcing that his father has been shot. He picks up the paper and stares at it; on reading the line, "They don't say if he's dead or alive," Pacino's voice quavers and cracks like a teenage boy's, underscoring this as a pivotal moment in Michael's maturity.

When Michael visits Vito at his hospital bed, Pacino conveys through his gaze—a Stravinsky-influenced, trancelike stare—that he understands that life as he knew it, as a civilian, is over. "I'm with you now," he tells his dad, though Michael's transition from innocent to Mafia don is a long way from complete. In the subsequent scene in which he, his brothers, and his father's men plot the murder of a cop, Pacino relays the plan in an affected voice that's almost reminiscent

of Humphrey Bogart—you get the sense that Michael is playing the part of the crook. But when the rest of the men in the room laugh as Michael squawks, "Who says you can't kill a cop?" Pacino remains stone-faced, embodying Michael's line, "It's strictly business."

After showing what he's capable of (to the audience, to his family, to himself), acting as the gunman in the job he plotted, Michael retreats to Sicily, where he starts a new life, even marrying a local girl, Apollonia (Simonetta Stefanelli). In this sequence—a kind of neorealist mini-film within the film—Michael buys into the illusion that the fate he was born into is something he can escape, and Pacino breaks out of the "trance," allowing the character to display what seems like genuine joy. But then Michael's wife is killed, by a car bomb meant for him. He realizes the danger she's in just a moment before the bomb goes off, screams out, "No! Apollonia, no!" and begins to lunge toward the car, but is thrown back by the force of the explosion. In this brief emotionally unguarded moment, Pacino suddenly cranks his volume and intensity to its limit. When Michael is at his most vulnerable, the nadir of his power, Pacino's performance reaches the top of its crescendo.

Resigned to his fate as a member of his family, Michael returns to New York, and we come to understand how fully he has given himself to his birthright by how deeply Pacino seems to have sunk back into that trance. Told that his brother Sonny has been killed, Michael strategically conceals any sign of emotion. Then he tracks down Kay, whom he apparently hasn't spoken to in years, and asks to get back together. "What's important, Kay, is that we have children," he says—a line Pacino delivers in a near-monotone that's somehow both somber and menacing.

The film moves incredibly quickly in its second half—years elapse in the space of a cut—and Pacino reveals less feeling with every passing scene. By the end, when Michael is lying to Kay about his involvement in his brother-in-law's murder, Pacino has suppressed any trace of the young man who told her, "That's my family, Kay. That's not me." Now, the family is, unquestionably, who he is.

Pacino has taken the character from apparent hero to a shell of a human being, the opposite of the inarticulate but visibly emotional male figures perfected by previous American Method actors such as James Dean and Marlon Brando. Here Pacino employs the Method taught to him by Lee Strasberg—not to dramatize the internal pain of the everyman but to apply a similar level of verisimilitude to a character who does the unspeakable, all the while keeping his feelings to himself. What's affecting about the performance is often not what he's doing but what he's not doing—the facial expression that remains fixed in the wake of a terrible revelation, the vocal tone

that fails to waver in the midst of a life-or-death negotiation. The crescendo Pacino performs in *The Godfather* introduces us to one of the fundamental tragedies of Michael Corleone's character, something Pacino would draw on in future performances: a man in control of his situation, personal or professional, does not need to show emotion.

A Conversation Between Actor and Director

The reviews were generally ecstatic. Pauline Kael's assessment of Pacino's achievement was typical: "Pacino creates a quiet, ominous space around himself; his performance is marvellous, too, big yet without ostentation... you don't catch him acting, yet he manages to change from a small, dosh-faced, darkly handsome college boy into an underworld lord, becoming more intense, smaller, and more isolated at every step."[33]

Pacino gave credit to his director: "With Francis, although I had personality differences with him, those were his performances, he *made* them. And he knew it. He'd say, 'I created you—you're my Frankenstein monster.'"[34] But Coppola the mad scientist was also open to input from his star. As Pacino recalled, "I went to Francis Ford Coppola with a list of things that I had to say after seeing the movie. He read the list. He considered it. He made some changes." He added, "The actor has something to offer; after all,

that's his trade. He may know just a little bit more about dialogue than the director, since that's what he does." Coppola would later describe his working relationship with Pacino as an ongoing conversation: "I tend to have a running stream of dialogue with Al, telling him how I feel, what's gone on before, more or less random thoughts, knowing he will seize on something that's helpful and disregard what isn't. Al is one of the most intelligent actors I've ever worked with."[35]

In two years, Pacino had gone from being the unwanted unknown begrudgingly cast to a major star whose participation could make or break the sequel. He was doubtful that he wanted to make the film, until a meeting with Coppola changed his mind. "Francis told me about the script," Pacino said. "He was so wigged out by the prospect of doing it, he would inspire anybody. The hairs on my head stood up. You can feel that sometimes with a director. I usually say, if you feel that with a director, go with him."[36] That Pacino's salary on the picture was slated at $600,000 plus 10 percent of the film's profits was an added incentive.

The Godfather Part II: The Bounce Is Gone

At the end of *The Godfather*, Michael promises Kay that "in five years, the Corleone family is going to be completely legitimate." It's not an empty promise—it's what his father wanted, for Michael to transcend underground, criminal

power and become an aboveboard power in the
legitimate world. "Senator Corleone. Governor
Corleone. Something," Vito says, to which Michael
responds, "We'll get there, Pop. We'll get there."
The Godfather Part II is the story of how Michael
tries to keep his promise to his wife and to his
father, but stumbles, destroying his home life and,
by killing his brother Fredo (John Cazale),
tragically altering the family he was born into.

The Godfather Part II opens with a shot of
Michael receiving a kiss on his ring, followed by
the image of an empty chair with an indentation
in its back. Michael Corleone, the new Don, is
struggling to fill the space left by his late father,
while keeping his two families together. The
domestic family is threatened first by an attempt
on Michael's life in his marital bedroom, and
eventually undone by what Kay refers to as
Michael's "blindness" in matters of the heart.
Michael's travails are interwoven with flashbacks
to the story of young Vito Corleone (Robert
De Niro), who flees Italy as a young boy after
witnessing his mother's murder, settles in the
Little Italy section of New York, and slowly rises
to power in the neighborhood's underworld,
eventually returning to Italy to enact revenge for
his mother's death.

Given Pacino's continued trancelike approach
to playing Michael as a man whose power stems
from his inscrutability and detachment, the
Vito storyline seems to function as a broadcast

of Michael's rumination on how he and his family
got to this point, of what his father's chair means
and how best to fill it. "At the end of *Part One*
there's a kind of bounce to Michael, that subtle
joy of what he's doing, that newness," Pacino said.
"In *Part Two*, he's been doing it for five years, and
the bounce has gone. That's what I went for."[37]

Again the film begins with a family event—
a lavish party at the new Corleone compound in
Nevada for Michael's son's first Communion—
that sketches the discrepancy between the
Godfather's public/family life and the business he
practices behind closed doors. While hordes dance
and eat in the garden, Michael meets in his office
with a Nevada senator who makes no secret of his
contempt for the Corleones. Responding to the
senator's proposal of blackmail, Pacino barely
speaks above a whisper, and the quieter he is, the
scarier. His show of power is seemingly effortless.

After establishing this power, the film then
presents Michael struggling to maintain his
composure when confronted with situations
beyond his control. After surviving a shoot-out
in his home, Michael travels to Havana to do
business with Hyman Roth, an aged Jewish
gangster (played by Pacino's mentor and dear
friend Lee Strasberg) who Michael suspects was
behind the attempt on his life. In the Havana
portion of the film, Michael is always observing,
often silently. Michael can't reveal his hand
to Roth—"I want him completely relaxed and

As a young boy, Al Pacino showed off his unconscious knack for Method acting by becoming physically sick when playing an ill actor in a school play—an achievement which earned him the playground nickname "Marlon Brando." To which Pacino called back, "Who's Marlon Brando?"[a] Pacino's introduction to his nick-namesake would come at age fourteen: transfixed by Brando's performance in *On the Waterfront*, the teenage Pacino sat through the movie twice.

While various versions of "The Method" had been percolating in American theater circles for decades, Marlon Brando was more strongly identified with the naturalistic, internalized performance style than any Hollywood star of his era. "There has been an American style of acting since Brando,"[b] Pacino would say of his costar in *The Godfather*. "We are all indebted to him."

On the set of *The Godfather*, Pacino drew confidence from Brando, who praised the younger actor's work early in the shoot and proved supportive throughout. But while Brando may have been inspirational to Pacino's development, as well as emotionally supportive, Pacino's approach to his character was introspective, not observational.

In other words, he wasn't looking to Brando for cues. "I don't feel I learn anything by watching," Pacino would say later. "I don't like to watch. Even in *The Godfather*, people ask, didn't you watch Brando? I said, 'No, I watch him when it's finished and on the screen.' I learn better and I learn more when I go through it and make the mistakes myself. Otherwise there's a tendency to avoid mistakes which might lead you someplace."[c]

Top: Kay and Michael have it out in *The Godfather Part II*.

Bottom: Diane Keaton and Al Pacino reprise their roles in *The Godfather Part III*.

confident in our friendship," he says — but without betraying emotion, Pacino uses his watchful eyes to tell the audience that the character is gathering information, attempting to sort out who's bluffing by reading faces as poker-ready as his own. Pacino plays Michael as a man who is constantly watching, and is well-aware that he is always being watched — Michael can't let any hint of his inner state slip out and be seen, and for the most part, Pacino skillfully keeps Michael's façade, rather than playing to the camera.

The exceptions, when Pacino foregrounds Michael's true feelings, are notable — and powerful. At a nightclub, during a cabaret act, Fredo drunkenly lets Michael overhear that he's well acquainted with Roth's lackey, Johnny Ola — a tacit admission that Fredo has been colluding behind his brother's back with the Jewish gangster who wants to eliminate Michael. Visibly affected by this news, Michael puts his hand over his mouth, as if revolted. In any other situation, this show of emotion on Michael's part would be considered huge. Coppola's camera reveals Pacino standing behind John Cazale's back, but the other characters in the scene are so distracted by a stage show that no one else seems to notice him. Michael keeps up appearances even as he's confronting the traitor. It's New Year's Eve, and the clock strikes twelve. Michael embraces his brother with a kiss on the mouth — showing their companions that all is well — and then whispers in his ear, "I know it was you, Fredo. You broke my heart. You broke my heart!"

Michael Corleone's Achilles' Heel

Michael's dealings with Fredo suggest a link between power and restraint — a subject that would run through all of Pacino's work and his artistry as an actor. As Michael Corleone, Pacino shows that when a man is in a position of power — and, perhaps more importantly, is comfortable in that position — he doesn't have to raise his voice. In fact, he barely needs to speak. The *Godfather* films suggest that an organization like the Mob, which essentially seeks to subvert the established social order, works most efficiently when it's silent and invisible to the outside observer. Outbursts are very clearly shown to be the refuge of a man out of options. In their final meeting before one brother kills the other, Fredo yells, — "I'm smart and I want respect!" — while Michael quietly, evenly informs his brother that their bond is broken.

But the pendulum swings the other way, too: there is a sharp contrast between how Michael handles a loss of control in business — which, to the Michael in *Part II*, includes Fredo's betrayal, although we'll see how the Michael of *Part III*

recasts this event as personal — and his inability to control what happens in his home. At the baptism party, Michael dances with his wife, Kay, who needles him about the promise he made to her at the end of the previous film: "...you once told me: 'In five years, the Corleone family will be completely legitimate.' That was seven years ago." Michael's response is weary, but tender: "I know. I'm trying, darling." At the very beginning of the film, Michael's success in wrestling control of the direction of the family business is thus linked to his success as a husband and a father. The points at which the two "family businesses" meet are generally points of failure. Pacino doesn't raise his voice until thirty minutes into the movie, after the assassination attempt — which, as he screams into a phone, takes place "in my bedroom, WHERE MY WIFE SLEEPS!"

The character's pivotal loss of control comes when Kay confronts him over the state of their union. Michael, unable to fathom that a wife would not stand by her husband no matter his actions, barely registers Kay's insistence that she's leaving him and taking the children. "No, I don't want to hear it!" he snaps. "I love you and I will not let you leave, because you are MINE!" Then he tries to regain his cool — and here the audience is conscious of Pacino the actor playing a man who is himself "acting," as Michael struggles to pull on his familiar mask of effortless control. "Don't you know me?" he asks his wife. "I would never let it happen; no, never, not if it took all my strength, all my cunning." "Oh, Michael," Kay says, seeing right through his act. "You are blind." Her recent miscarriage? "It wasn't a miscarriage; it was an abortion! Just like our marriage is an abortion!"

When Michael then hits Kay, it's genuinely shocking. In his performance, Pacino has created a man who we know is responsible for many murders, and yet he's also effectively sold him to us as a family man, whose criminal activity could be written off as collateral messiness necessary in order to achieve the greater good of keeping that promise of legitimacy to his father and his wife. With this violent outburst, Michael reveals the shallowness of that promise, and the limits of his control.

The Achilles' heel of Michael Corleone — a man who, as Pacino rightly put it, had a "bounce" when first given control of his family business — turns out to be the intersection of the professional and the personal, and failures on this fault line will reliably break his façade of impossible cool. These themes are pushed to the limit in *Part III*.

Caught in a Vise

The Godfather offered Pacino the chance to transform over the course of the film — a difficult task, but graspable as an actor, and readable to the audience, as a defined progression. *Part II* gave the actor an even harder task, providing less to work with in terms of narrative progression—he starts and ends as the head of the family. Coppola compared Pacino's acting challenge to "being caught in a vise... working on a much more subtle level, very rarely having a big climactic scene where an actor can unload, like blowing the spittle out of the tube of a trombone. The entire performance had to be kind of vague and so understated that, as an actor, you couldn't really be sure what you were doing."[38] The *Godfather Part II* shoot lasted twenty grueling weeks. "I was living with that weight all the time," Pacino later related, "and it was suffocating, it was hurting."[39]

On a pure performance level, the shoot was physically and emotionally draining, and the conditions of the production didn't help matters, either. Midway through, Pacino was diagnosed with bronchial pneumonia and hospitalized for ten days. "We were in the Dominican Republic, and I was being treated like a prince or something," he recalled. "Eight bodyguards and all, which was unnecessary. It was very disconcerting. I got physically ill. I was just overworking in that part."[40]

Pacino, who did not speak Spanish, used the sense of being lost in a foreign land to his advantage. "As an actor, you use everything that is true. The character, Michael Corleone, is visiting this foreign city, Havana, for the first time. He is on unfamiliar territory and can't even understand what people in the street are saying. Something seems to be going on and he's suspicious. Now, I understand that completely."[41]

The Godfather Part III: Back to the Future

Fifteen years passed between the release of *The Godfather Part II* and the beginning of production on *Part III*, for the simple reason that Coppola didn't want to make it. Coppola mused on the third film's DVD commentary that after making the first sequel, "There seemed to be nothing further to be said."[42] The franchise continued to be profitable for Paramount, and finally, in 1989, the studio offered Coppola carte blanche to make a third part any way he liked. What he chose to do was catch up with a Michael Corleone ready to confront his past and seek redemption. "We tried," Coppola said, "to deal with the cathartic themes of finally dealing with your life and coming to terms with your sins."[43]

While the first two *Godfather* films are origin stories, *Part III* plays like a *Godfather* saga greatest-hits reel, incorporating flashbacks both literally and figuratively. An aged Michael, in search of salvation and puzzled as to where his best laid plans went wrong, often thinks about the past, and Coppola presents this by cutting from a shot of Michael lost in thought to an image from the first or second installment—

an extension of the cross-cutting that made Vito's story play as though broadcast from Michael's mind in *Part II*. Coppola also invites the viewer to "flash back" by having characters refer to scenes from the previous two films (like when Kay meets Michael in Sicily and reminds him of the conversation about his family they had at Connie's wedding in the first *Godfather*) and through staging (an important assassination happens amidst the chaos of the San Gennaro festival, just as it did in the Vito section of *Part II*). In *Part III*, when Michael's daughter Mary is killed by a bullet meant for her father, we're instantly reminded of *The Godfather*, when Michael's first wife was killed by a car bomb meant for him. In that film, the sound of the explosion interrupted Michael's cry. This time, Pacino collapsed to his knees screaming, but sound designer Walter Murch took out the audio in post, making it, as Coppola noted, "much more agonizing."[44]

These tactics help imbue empathy into *Part III*'s Michael, who is unable to act effectively in the present, in part because the past has clouded his view of the future. The final images of *Part III* show Michael, apparently some years after the main action of the film, "coming to" after a long flashback to his glory days, and then dying horribly alone. The sequence recasts the whole trilogy as a dying man's nightmarish reverie of his past.

A New Strain

Michael's late-in-life introspection reflected where the director was at the time: having lost his eldest son in a boating accident in 1986, Coppola—like Michael, who is paralyzed with guilt for ordering the death of his brother Fredo and thus having "killed my mother's son"—was grappling with an older man's regrets. "I myself don't think about the future so much in the same way I did when I was young," Coppola said. "If you work hard or you've got a lotta dreams, you think in terms of winning, that you will realize your dreams. And when you lose a son like that, you realize you're lost. That you can't win."[45] The film is bookended by a letter Michael writes to his son and daughter begging for reconciliation, in which he says he's come to understand that "the only worth in this world is children," and Michael's lonely death, having apparently never recovered from the murder of his daughter Mary.

During the shoot, which began in November 1989 and lasted for ten months, Coppola and Pacino's working relationship was not as simpatico as it had once been. The problems started when Pacino showed up on set with his hair down to his shoulders; it took two weeks for Coppola to convince his star that a short, silvery do was more appropriate for the sixty-something Michael. Pacino also second-guessed the rewrites required by the absence of Robert Duvall, who could not be convinced to work for what

Paramount was willing to pay him, as well as the last-minute casting of Sofia Coppola as Mary, a role originally meant for Winona Ryder. "I think it's difficult when you cast your own kid," Pacino stated after the film was released. "It was a strain. The film developed a strain. I think there was a problem in the fabric of the story, but I wish that we'd had the complete cast."[46] Adding to the strain, Coppola continued to rewrite the script throughout production, even changing the ending at the last minute so that Mary would die instead of Michael, something the studio would have preferred. At one point during the shoot, an angry Pacino phoned James Caan to vent about Coppola. "It was not the Francis who did the first *Godfather*," admitted Caan in 1992.[47]

But it was not the same Pacino who did the first *Godfather*, either. "I didn't know if I could be that guy again," Pacino admitted.[48] Yet, as a stage-trained actor who hadn't planned to become a movie star, he understood the character as a man who "had a desire to do something else and was taken off his course and put on another course. The moment when he made the decision to go in that direction has been the thing he has dealt with his entire life."[49]

Out of Control

Indeed, the Al Pacino who plays Michael Corleone in *The Godfather Part III* seems totally different from the one who played him nearly twenty years earlier. Pacino's performance in the first two *Godfather* films is a marvel of vocal precision: his Michael, the sole college-educated Corleone, speaks carefully, his diction noticeably neat compared to Brando's mumbling, his New York accent faint compared to Caan's or Cazale's. In *Part III*, Pacino's voice is audibly hoarse, his accent unmistakably present, his cadences softened. Michael's voice surely would have been ravaged by age, stress, and sickness, but here Pacino simply doesn't sound like an aged version of the Michael Corleone he created—he sounds like Al Pacino. Though he launched his film career with this role that relied so heavily on restraint and calculated explosion, Pacino had two decades later established a star persona based on characters remembered for their outbursts— Serpico, Tony Montana in *Scarface*, *Dog Day Afternoon*'s Sonny. In the past he had complained that the Paramount executives didn't understand his understated approach to the character, that Coppola had wanted him to "do more." Now "doing more" was simply his default.

In *Part II*, Michael was conscious that any emotion he allowed on his face or in his voice could be used against him; he mostly manages to exercise restraint in a business context, but his inability to keep his cool with Kay costs him his marriage. No matter which way Michael swings, Pacino almost never gives the viewer information

that's unavailable to the other characters in a given scene. In *Part III*, it's impossible not to see Al Pacino the actor playing to the camera. This is both a detriment to our suspension of disbelief and a fitting performance strategy, in that Michael, too, is losing the incredible mastery over his "mask" that we've seen him exercise in the previous films. Early in *Part III*, Kay alludes to the hypocrisy of the old Michael's approach: "Let's be reasonable," she says coolly. "That's your big thing, isn't it? Reason? Backed by murder?" Late in life, the Godfather counsels the generation biting his heels to keep their passions in check—cautioning his protégé and illegitimate nephew, Vincent, to "never let anyone know what you're thinking" and explaining to his daughter Mary the tragedy of his lusty first marriage, in the hope that it'll cure her of her incestuous love for her cousin. But Michael rarely follows his own advice. The Michael of *Part III* is a man whose public and inner selves have long been radically at odds with each other, and as he ages he's losing the ability to keep his two competing natures in check.

Part of the problem is that while Michael can claim to have transformed the Corleone family business into a "legitimate" one, it's a constant struggle to keep the family's criminal legacy from bubbling to the surface. After an attempt to shut other Mob families out of a business deal results in a massacre that he only narrowly escapes, Michael is forced to confront the tenuousness of his business "legitimacy," and of his own power. The film's most famous scene allows Pacino to put an eye-bulging, crescendoing stamp on what would become a catchphrase: "Just when I thought I was out, they pull. Me. Back. IN." This line reading, with its unlikely syncopation and unusual emotional transparency, would have been unthinkable coming from the "old" Michael, who kept such private ruminations unsaid, even to those closest to him. That the scene ends with Michael suffering a diabetic stroke makes it absolutely clear that he has not practiced what he preached. Now there's no hiding that Michael's position in power is as precarious as his health.

Al Pacino was in a somewhat better place than the man he played, but his future was nonetheless uncertain. It had been a decade and a half since his fame peaked with *Dog Day Afternoon*. *Sea of Love*, which opened in the US just two months before *Part III* started shooting, had been his first screen appearance following a four-year hiatus. The time away evidently aged him. While Pacino could have credibly played twenty-something well into his forties, in his fifties he was, as *Godfather* producer Peter Bart put it in 1997, no longer "clean faced and hungry" but now "convey[ed] the gravitas of a grizzled veteran."[50]

The changes in Pacino's screen presence were not merely physical. Pauline Kael had previously praised the fact that she wasn't able to "catch him acting." Now Pacino performed as if eager to be caught—or, at least, as though he was no longer interested in making viewers forget about their preconceived notions of the Pacino persona. Coppola plays with the viewer's awareness of Pacino's body of work through the character of Vincent, played by Andy Garcia, whose resemblance to a younger Al Pacino acted as a pointer to the first *Godfather* film. Meanwhile, Vincent's highly sexualized, violent loose-cannon bravado seems influenced by Pacino's near-camp performance in *Scarface*. In Michael's relationship with Vincent, and in the film's structure as a subjective view of past and present through the eyes of a survivor mystified over time lost, *Part III* literally puts the Pacino of 1990 in dialogue with his earlier self. It makes sense that we recognize Pacino as being separate from Michael: while the character he plays confronts his past, Pacino, by now a calcified personality on screen, is forced through the magic of editing to confront his fresh-faced youth with a combination of romantic nostalgia and wizened remorse. For the actor who played Michael, *The Godfather Part III* functioned as a settling of old accounts, a way of introducing his new self to the Pacino of memory, reconciling the two in order to move on to a very different future.

But if Pacino, like Michael, had been counting on this final return to the well for redemption, it didn't quite work out as planned. *Godfather III* was not universally well received by critics, nor did it dominate the pop-cultural conversation the way the previous films in the trilogy had. The world had changed in a decade and a half—and, certainly, Hollywood had changed—but Michael Corleone had changed, too. Once his promotional duties were over, Pacino didn't hide his frustration over how *Part III* had turned out. "You know what the problem with that film was? The real problem?" he asked in 2005. "Nobody wanted to see Michael have retribution and feel guilty."

Maybe that was a problem for the *Godfather* fans who, through repeat viewings on television and VHS, had memorized the Michael Corleone of the first two films, the impenetrable, untouchable antihero, and couldn't stand to see him change. Or maybe the film was doomed because of the unprecedented level of anticipation surrounding it. Regardless, at age fifty, Pacino was still in search of respectability. He would find it two years later by winning the Oscar for *Scent of a Woman*—a "victory" that would make some fans long for the "common Mafia hood" Pacino had left behind. In a sense, every accolade Pacino receives seems like a belated nod to the enormity of his *Godfather* accomplishment. It's a double-edged sword: Pacino's Michael Corleone is almost certainly the greatest performance by an actor in an American blockbuster movie, but its sheer quality has set a standard that Pacino himself has long struggled to match, let alone beat.

2

Francis "Lion" Delbuchi

Scarecrow (1973)
Jerry Schatzberg

"A crow isn't afraid of a scarecrow. It laughs."
—Lion

After filming *The Godfather*, Al Pacino was on the brink of stardom to a degree he never imagined—and wasn't particularly interested in. His anxiety over the larger-than-life version of himself he associated with movie stardom manifested itself the night of the *Godfather* premiere, when Pacino was forced to confront the literally larger-than-life image of himself on the big screen. He had seen a rough cut of the film, but he was unprepared for the experience of watching it with a crowd. A few minutes after arriving, he fled. "At the premiere, I was drunk," he admitted later. "The lights went down and I just had to get out. Seeing yourself with a lot of people—it's tough."[51]

With *The Godfather*'s success, Pacino could have taken the careerist route of moving to LA, or otherwise exploited his celebrity in New York. Instead, Pacino slunk back into his nourishing comfort zone: the theater. Pacino headed to Boston to star in a David Wheeler production of *The Basic Training of Pavlo Hummel*. "I thought it would help me avoid the impact of the film, if I had something to concentrate on," Pacino said.[52]

An outsider to the film industry before *The Godfather*, Pacino's resistance to the celebrity his triumph in that landmark achievement offered marked him as a self-styled iconoclast, but also a coward: his flight from the *Godfather* premiere suggests that it was easier for him to remove himself from the situation than to stay and figure out how to embrace it. It's no small wonder that for his next screen role Pacino chose a character who has dropped out of mainstream society, for whom the notion of doing the "normal" thing—fulfilling the expectations for a man of his station—is something he's never been able to do.

A "Real" Road Movie

Scarecrow, helmed by Pacino's *Panic in Needle Park* director Jerry Schatzberg, from a script by first-time screenwriter Garry Michael White, is a loosely plotted character study focusing on the cross-country travels of two drifters. Max (Gene Hackman) is a burly, tempestuous bullshit artist, fresh out of prison, carrying a single valise and wearing everything else he owns in four or five layers on his body. Francis Lionel Delbuchi (Pacino), small and apparently imperturbably good-natured, has just finished a stint in the merchant marines. The two strangers have both ended up on a deserted stretch of rural California highway with their thumbs out, looking to hitchhike east. At first rivals for a ride on opposite sides of the street, they end up in the back of the same truck, and by the time they finish breakfast the next morning, Max has given Francis a new name—"Lion"—and has invited his new friend to take part in his dreamed-of business venture, a car wash in Pittsburgh. Max has money in a bank there; his plan is to make his way to his new home, stopping near Denver to see his sister. Lion cheerfully agrees to Max's plan, as long as they can also stop in Detroit on the way—he's carrying a lamp, a gift for the five-year-old son he's never met and whose conception prompted him to sail away.

Shot on location on the roads connecting America's two coasts—and the small towns, big cities, and rural non-places in between—*Scarecrow* gave Pacino a chance to disappear into a character, far from the uncomfortable spotlights shined by the media in Los Angeles and New York. To get into character, Pacino spent a week with Hackman dressed as a hobo, panhandling on the streets of San Francisco. "This early experience at cadging quarters from street people and copping of cigar butts from the gutters paid off in stark realism when Schatzberg's hidden camera followed them through the streets of Reno, Nevada, Denver and Canon City, Colorado, and Detroit, Michigan, plus a score of smaller towns along the way"—or so claimed Warner Bros.' glossy press brochure produced to promote *Scarecrow*'s release. "All kinds of people laid bread on us," Pacino recalled. "We picked up about four bucks in less than an hour. One department store made us check our shopping bags at the door and another one put the house dick on our tails and gave us the bum's rush back out onto the street."[53]

Pacino's Method training dictated that this kind of lived experience would help the actor in terms of authenticating his performance, providing memories from which to draw on in creating the emotional life of Lion. But this "authenticity" was produced via highly contrived circumstances. Pacino and Hackman's

Al Pacino as Francis "Lion" Delbuchi in Jerry Schatzberg's *Scarecrow* (1973).

panhandling was temporary and not motivated
by need, and was thus a performance in itself,
a burlesque of the bum's life. In fact, at times
Scarecrow plays like an acting exercise that
Schatzberg's camera happened to capture. This
is actually fitting in that the film is ultimately
very much about acting—the performances its
characters put on in public as well as acting as
an external means of expressing internal feeling
and action. With Hackman and Pacino trading
off as performer and spectator, the film shows
the two men become indivisible partners, while
continuously watching how the other enacts
a specific type of masculinity. *Scarecrow* explores
"acting" both as in performance and as in taking
decisive action by tracking two men who are
fluent in the former variety but incapable of the
latter. In the end, one man is able to muster the
ability to take action when the other loses his
ability to maintain the act that has sustained him.

A Film About Performance

The first line of dialogue in *Scarecrow* comes out
of Pacino's mouth, a few minutes into the movie.
We've just watched Hackman's Max literally
fall on his ass, after having tangled himself in
a barbed-wire fence while trying to cross from
an empty field to a faceless rural American
highway. Pacino, standing on the other side of
the street, has witnessed this, too—from behind

a tree. Schatzberg cuts back and forth between
the two actors to stress the point that, intentionally
or not, within the scene, one man is performing
and the other is choosing not to intervene—not
to act himself, but instead to observe. Only when
the "show" is over does one man address the
other. "How you doin'?" Pacino's Francis calls
across the street. "You okay?"

Max doesn't answer, which Francis sees as
his cue to take up the mantle of performance—
it's a tool used by Pacino's character, and
eventually Hackman's, to break down defenses.
Still across the street, and still a stranger,
Francis tries to attract and hold Max's attention
through an extraordinary show of action—
bouncing up and down, imitating a monkey, and
finally pantomiming a phone call with an unseen,
unidentified (and, of course, nonexistent) other.
This act is so loony, so go-for-broke, that Max
can't resist. Francis's display calls to mind the
playground antics of a young Pacino who used
his ability to make peers laugh to smooth over
his social anxiety. Indeed, the initial bond between
the two men is that both have a tough time fitting
into society's definition of "normal" adult male
behavior. Max's response to his own deficiency
is to overcompensate by imposing his manly
prerogative on anyone weak enough to be domi-
nated by him—which leads to excessive drinking,
womanizing, and brawling. Francis goes the
other way, diffusing any potentially awkward

situation with childlike jesting. Both instincts are demonstrated when Max insists on renaming his new buddy "Lion"—after his middle name, Lionel, with the implication that a friend of Max's needs a name more masculine than "Francis"—and Francis accepts this rebranding cheerfully, like it's a game of pretend.

His teeth then straight and perfectly white, Pacino likely smiles more in this, his third starring role, than in any film he's made since. For much of *Scarecrow*, Pacino seems to be the film's light, affable, and imperturbable heart, almost its comic relief. He radiates simple, good-natured warmth. While later Pacino characters would, to paraphrase his Vincent Hanna from *Heat*, hold on to and even feed off their own angst, Lion seems blissfully—maybe even suspiciously—angst-free.

The film's title comes from a story that Pacino's character tells his new friend suggesting that a scarecrow doesn't actually "scare" crows at all, but instead makes them laugh—and so predators and enemies can be mellowed, even turned into friends, through clowning rather than hostility. Spouting this potentially too-cute life lesson and then teaching Max by example, Lion seems like he could be a cipher, there to school the irascible, gruff, and bad-tempered Max to make life easier for himself by being less of an overbearing personality.

But the scarecrow theory is tested again and again. In one bar scene, Lion first dances with

Max to distract him from the latter's romantic rival, then leads the whole bar in drunken, goofball revelry—but Max breaks the spell by instigating a brawl. That fight gets both Lion and Max thrown into a work camp, where Lion tries to diffuse the threat of a sexual advance from another man, Riley, by joking. With the larger Riley physically closing in on him, Lion tosses out a *Frankenstein* reference—"Igor, you crazy monster!"—a strangely revealing reflex that betrays the horror behind Lion's smile. It's the wrong move. Riley thinks Lion is laughing at him, and scarecrow Lion is badly beaten by his seducer.

In *Scarecrow*'s pivotal scene, we see Hackman's Max attempting to apply the lessons he's learned from Pacino's Lion, with unexpected results. Released from the camp, the men end up in another bar, with Max, as usual, close to fisticuffs with a stranger. Drunk, Lion withdraws, and the student gleefully tries to cheer up his despondent master by punching a nudie-club classic into the jukebox and performing a striptease. This forces Lion, heretofore the film's proponent of and source of comic relief, to confront himself and his own worldview for the first time. He doesn't like what he sees. The long shot on Pacino that closes this scene indicates to audiences that the clown's mask is just that—a mask—and there's much more to Lion than we've seen.

The idea that Lion has been hiding his true self is hammered home in *Scarecrow*'s climactic

Cambridge Dictionary defines Method acting as "a style of acting in which an actor tries to understand and feel the emotions of the character he or she represents."[d]

In practice, Method acting has come to mean different things to different people, including its teachers and practitioners.

Most can agree that the Method is indebted to the teachings of Russian realist-theater pioneer Constantin Stanislavski, who developed a "System" designed to make actors intensely involved in the conception of characters by bringing their own memories and experiences to the material. Stanislavski's teachings were popularized in the United States by actor-turned-teacher Lee Strasberg. In the 1930s, inspired by the Moscow Art Theater, Strasberg founded the Group Theatre with Harold Clurman and Cheryl Crawford. This group evolved into the Actors Studio, which, with Strasberg as artistic director, was the crucible for the Method that would make its way to Hollywood via stars like James Dean, Marilyn Monroe, and Al Pacino. Strasberg was drawn to the Stanislavski style for its ability to convey realism. Of the Moscow Art Theater, he marveled, "Every actor on the stage, no matter how small or insignificant his role, was equally real, equally believable, equally convincing."[e]

At the Actors Studio, Strasberg instilled techniques like improvisation and affective memory (also called "substitution") to teach actors to bring the vitality of lived experience to the static text of the script. An actor using the Strasberg Method might, for example, prepare for a scene featuring a character in mourning by recalling what it felt like when someone close to him died in real life; if he didn't have a death to draw on, the actor would try to substitute the memory of another event that made him feel comparative sorrow. The Method was merely the means to the end, aiming for, to quote the Lee Strasberg Theatre and Film Institute, "the (re)experiencing of life by the actor within the fiction of the story as if it were true and happening now."[f]

Several of Strasberg's collaborators eventually diverged from the Actors Studio to promote different versions of the Method. Stella Adler had been an original member of the Group Theatre, but after training with Stanislavski (becoming the only American actor to do so), Adler decided Strasberg was misinterpreting Stanislavski's teachings, and she eventually started her own school. Instead of relying on lived memory, Adler advocated that an actor closely study the script and extrapolate the character from the text, using external tools—voices and accents, body language, props and costuming, technical training—to spark emotional response and imagination. While there is some overlap between the exercises and techniques involved in the Strasberg and Adler Methods, the basic difference between their two philosophies is that while Strasberg believed an actor should shape the character to feelings and experiences familiar to the performer, Adler believed it was the actor's job to immerse himself in the character as dictated on the page. Her students included Brando, De Niro, Judy Garland, and Warren Beatty. Like Adler, original Group Theatre member and Actors Studio teacher Sanford Meisner came to believe that Strasberg's techniques caused an actor to focus on himself to the detriment of the script and the context of the scene; his Meisner Technique focused on exercises promoting truthful reaction. Robert Lewis, another Strasberg follower turned dissident, also thought basing characters on lived experience and memory was too limiting, and advocated extensive vocal training. Strasberg himself would eventually disdain the use of the term "the Method," which he felt implied "a set of hard and fast rules which is precisely the opposite of what I believe in. You can't give actors rules to follow— like apprentice plumbers. The question Stanislavski addressed himself was this: 'Where does an actor's imagination start?'... That is the heart of what has been called the 'method.' It is a working technique through which an actor expands and disciplines his imagination."[g]

Top: Stella Adler addresses actors at the Stella Adler Studio of Acting in 1984.

Bottom: A lesson at the Actors Studio in 1955. Seated in the first row are James Dean and Lee Strasberg (center).

fountain scene. Having finally arrived in Detroit, Lion calls his abandoned wife, Annie (played by Charlie Laughton's wife, Penny Allen) before stopping in to see her and meet his son. Though there is a kid who looks like a dead ringer for Al Pacino at age five playing in her apartment, Annie angrily tells Lion that she miscarried their son, in an accident that he could have prevented had he not skipped town. Lion is clearly devastated by this information. But after hanging up the phone, he puts on a high-energy happy face to greet Max and makes up a lie about why it's no longer necessary to go visit his kid. The two end up at a public fountain, where Max drinks from a paper bag, and Lion innocently clowns for a group of neighborhood kids. Then, without warning, something snaps; Lion hoists one of the kids up on his shoulders and wades into the ice-cold fountain. Reeling from Annie's harsh words, he loses his ability to put on a happy face, and suffers a catatonic breakdown. Lion is hospitalized, and the film ends with Max embarking on the final leg to Pittsburgh alone with the promise to return with his car wash money to pay for his shattered friend's treatment. Lion and Max's road trip, the process through which they attempt to settle old debts and claim their chunk of the postwar American dream, is derailed before they reach their destination. Half a decade after *Easy Rider*, *Scarecrow* reconfirms that the myth of the American road as a blank slate for renewal is a sham.

Pacino vs. Hackman

"We started filming in Bakersfield, California, and traveled cross-country, shooting all the way to Detroit in absolute continuity," Hackman remembered in 2005. "That's something you almost never get to do."[54] So a road trip shot in sequence allowed the actors—who, despite floating around the same New York stage world orbit and Hackman's having been the roommate of Pacino's old rival Dustin Hoffman, had not previously met—to get to know each other as the characters did. Pacino also got to know Hackman's brother, Richard, who played a small role in the film. Pacino and the other Hackman became drinking buddies, sitting in with local bar bands until the wee hours of the morning, even on nights before early call times.

But whereas Max and Lion start out as strangers and become intimate companions, the actors playing them never developed such a rapport. "We had to play a very close relationship, but I just didn't think we were as connected as we should have been," Pacino admitted. "We seemed apart. We didn't have altercations, but we didn't communicate, didn't think in the same terms. We didn't hate each other, but I had a stronger connection to Brando."[55]

Pacino biographer Andrew Yule inferred from his subject's diplomatic quote that "there were in fact constant altercations among Pacino, Hackman and Schatzberg—in between the bouts of silence, that is." Yule suggests that the friction may have had something to do with simple actorly egotism and competition— as Yule writes, both actors were aware that "Hackman indisputably had the showier role and therefore stood a far greater chance of dominating the film than Pacino." He goes on to cite that pivotal bar scene in which Hackman "all but consumes the furniture as he hilariously performs a striptease, coyly removing endless items of his on-the-road apparel, while the other occupants of the bar cheer him on—and Pacino beholds the spectacle disbelievingly. 'Why ain't I doin' that?' his bemused expression seems to suggest."[56]

But *Scarecrow* and the dynamic between its stars are much more complicated than Yule gives them credit for. While Hackman does indeed dominate the first half of the film, in its second half, *Scarecrow*'s narrative seesaws toward Pacino. That striptease is, without question, the key scene of the movie, but not because Pacino, as Yule seems to suggest, slips out of character to bare his jealousy. In White's original script, this scene was clearly intended to focus on Max's transformation, rather than Lion's. "We see Max, now as Lion, his conversion complete," White writes at the end of the scene, "responding to the humanity of laughter."[57] In the finished film, the funda-mental meaning of the scene is changed by the long shot contemplating Pacino's troubled face, which makes it plain that *Scarecrow* is Lion's story, the tragedy of a man who tried to outrun his past mistakes and move forward with a smile on his face, only to learn that the past is inescapable. In other words, through Hackman's striptease, we come to understand that Pacino's character is not a supporting, sidekick presence to Hackman's antihero—instead, Lion is the heart of the movie.

It's possible that the choice to include Pacino's reaction shot was not a creative decision on the part of director Schatzberg. "I had a problem with Al," Schatzberg revealed at a *Scarecrow* screening in 2011. "His manager [Marty Bregman] told him that it was not his film and he believed it." The director admitted to making a few changes in the editing room because "Al said he'd like to see the camera favor him more."[58] For better or worse, this is another early example of Pacino proving to be the auteur of his own career, first by making a statement with his choice of role, then by giving a perfor-mance that aimed to achieve a level of realism by drawing on lived experience, and finally by exerting pressure on the way that role came together in the editing room.

Notions of Manhood

The striptease scene is also where the subtext of Max and Lion's relationship, that it has transcended mere fraternity, becomes text, with one referring to the other as "my wife." They are like an old couple, their deepened relationship no longer just a matter of traveling convenience.

The near-romantic dynamic between the two men was a major topic of conversation at the time of the film's release. Hackman and Pacino were pegged as part of a trend of boy-boy on-screen pairings that rivaled the intimacy of the boy-girl couples of classical Hollywood. Many reviews cited Leslie Fiedler, the literary critic who made the case that the male friendships of American fiction were infused with unspoken romantic tension. From the beginning of *Scarecrow*, wrote Joy Gould Boyum in the *Wall Street Journal*, "We know that [Max and Lion] are destined to become still another couple in the tradition of Natty Bumppo and Chingachgook, of Huck Finn and Jim, of Lennie and George, of Captain America and Billy, of Ratso and Joe Buck. This last overtone is somewhat unfortunate since it enforces Al Pacino's natural tendency to remind us of Dustin Hoffman and works against the distinctiveness of his performance."[59] Pacino had been battling off claims of his physical resemblance to the other actor since his theater days—a testament to how unprepared critics were at the time to see short, dark actors with naturalistic styles on American screens—but it didn't help that Hoffman's performance as a margin-dweller in the Best Picture–winning *Midnight Cowboy* (John Schlesinger, 1969) still lingered in the collective consciousness.

Scared Away

Scarecrow won the Palme d'Or at the 1973 Cannes Film Festival, but back in the States it struck out at the box office and wasn't appreciated by critics, who tapped into something amiss about the production. "Technical credits are all tops—perhaps a shade too professional, too slick, too contrasting with the authentic gritty locales sought out by the filmmakers," wrote staff reviewer "Murf" at *Variety*.[60] The *Hollywood Reporter* critic Alan R. Howard was more direct: "Its naturalism is too synthetic and its drama unconvincing."[61]

"Here's a picture that manages to abuse two prime American myths at once—the Road and the Male Pair," wrote Stanley Kauffmann, one of *Scarecrow*'s most vicious detractors, in the *New Republic*. After bashing the film's "fake symbolic realism," the critic went on to dismiss its star as miscast. "Pacino proves, to those who needed proof, that he is good only for menace; and this role has no menace."[62]

Kauffmann's review suggests that he missed the arc of the film, or perhaps just stepped out during Pacino's terrifying fountain breakdown. *Scarecrow*'s "abuse" of those "prime American myths" was, of course, intentional—the movie seeks not to celebrate the givens of American mythology but to deconstruct them. *Scarecrow*'s characters not only never reach the end of the line—the film seems to suggest that there is no such thing as closure, that "the end of the line," like the horizon on the American road, is always in sight and yet permanently out of reach.

Oddly enough, Pacino agreed with the critics. "*Scarecrow* was the saddest experience of my career," he admitted in 1979. His explanation implied lingering frustration with Schatzberg and the film's studio, Warner Bros. "That was a definite example of negligence. It was the greatest script I ever read… Because people wanted to come in below budget, we sacrificed the movie. There were scenes deleted."[63]

In time, *Scarecrow* would come to be considered Schatzberg's masterpiece. The film is frequently revived in New York, and in 2005, over thirty years after its original theatrical run, it was finally released on DVD, opening the door for new appraisals. Critic Dave Kehr would make the case that *Scarecrow*'s vision of manhood looked better with age, in that it offered a much-needed correction to the blank, homogenous fantasies of masculinity promoted by contemporary movies. "That their vague dreams will never be fulfilled is a given; the film belongs to a time, now long past, when American movies still interested themselves in losers and the socially marginalized, rather than the pumped-up triumphalists Tom Cruise has come to embody."[64]

But back in 1973, it was hard to see *Scarecrow* as a success. Pacino left the production in no particular hurry to add to his screen résumé. He instead returned to David Wheeler's Theatre Company of Boston, where he'd take his first stab at a character that would become central to his own process of self-examination: Richard III.

3 Frank Serpico

Serpico (1973)
Sidney Lumet

"I have never stayed in any political arenas. It was just not my thing. The sociopolitical aspects of the films I make are never the front-runner in my mind. It's always the story, the character." —Al Pacino, 1979

Al Pacino's admission that he has never been a political person calls to mind a phrase popularized around the time he started making movies: the personal *is* political.[65] For a stretch, beginning with *Scarecrow* in 1973 and ending with *Cruising* in 1980, Pacino made continuous statements about the world he lived in by choosing roles in films that tapped into a certain collective disillusionment within the culture, a distrust of authority, and a feeling of the futility of the individual in conflict with the rotten status quo. Pacino spent the decade playing cops and criminals who blurred the lines between hero and villain, men whose divided natures embodied the confusion and ambiguity of modern American life, and particularly the changing notions of masculinity. He solidified his Hollywood stardom through a series of roles in which he embodied the everyman oppressed by the system, a kind of superhero from the streets who could fulfill the viewer's fantasies of fighting back. If you had to pick a single word to sum up his screen persona of the 1970s—quite arguably the strongest decade of his career—that word would have to be "resistance."

Scarecrow may have started this run by calling the basics of the American Dream into question, but despite its success in Europe, the film was barely seen by Americans. The concept of Pacino as an icon of resistance was really introduced and cemented by a core of three films: *Serpico*, *Dog Day Afternoon*, and *...And Justice for All*. *Serpico*—the actor's first solo-billing-above-the-title star vehicle—established the self-professed politically agnostic actor as an avatar for every American male who felt disenfranchised by the broken system. He was once again proving to be the auteur of his own career by choosing roles that spoke to the free-floating anxiety in the culture.

Serpico: A Bespoke Production

In her dismissal of *Serpico*, *New Yorker* critic Pauline Kael noted that actors liked to work with the film's director, Sidney Lumet, "because he lets them do what they want."[66] In fact, in the case of *Serpico*, the goal of the picture was to build itself around Al Pacino's wants and needs— including adjusting the shooting schedule based on the looming *Godfather Part II* start date. *Serpico* was literally tailor-made for its star, from conception to postproduction—Pacino even sat in on editing until *The Godfather Part II* called him away.

Marty Bregman, still Pacino's manager and now the head of upstart production company Artists Entertainment Complex, had his sights set on casting his client in a film adaptation of Peter Maas's 1973 biography of real-life New York cop Frank Serpico.

John G. Avildsen was initially hired to direct the film, but after insisting on shooting in the real Serpico's childhood home—a logistical nightmare—Avildsen was forced out and Sidney Lumet brought in. By 1972, Lumet could have been justifiably called a veteran—his résumé directing stage, TV, and film productions dated back to the early 1950s—but he was hardly considered an auteur. He had a reputation for efficiency, one which he made good on with *Serpico*: Lumet wrapped the picture in just fifty-one days, and three months after the completion of shooting, the movie was in theaters. Unlike Avildsen, Lumet wasn't one to make stylistic decisions that would overwhelm the material. The one common thread running through his highly diverse body of work was strong support for actors, allowing them to put personal stamps on their performances through intensive rehearsals. Improvisation, felt Lumet, "can be an effective tool in rehearsal as a way of finding out what you're really like when, for example, you're angry. Knowing your feelings lets you know when those feelings are real as opposed to simulating them."[67] *Serpico* would be nothing if not a showcase for a big, bold performance from a star aiming for realism. "There are only a handful of actors who are literally incapable of doing anything false, and Al is one of them," Lumet declared. "He simply gets into character and doesn't come out."[68]

Points of Connection

In 1973, with three starring film roles under his belt, Al Pacino still thought of himself as a stage

actor who was finding his way around movie
sets, stumbling through the fragmented process
of creating a role for the camera. Explaining
the difference between the two types of acting to
a reporter that year, Pacino said, "I have a very
strong musical sense, and in a movie, there's no
chance for the rhythm to build." But in the theater,
"words are notes to me, and I play them."[69]

Just as he had panhandled to prepare for
Scarecrow, Pacino figured he should prepare to
play the part of Frank Serpico—a policeman who
bravely came forward to reveal corruption in his
own department and later survived a shooting
incident that may have been an attempt to shut
him up. "I went out with cops one night," he
remembered, "did about five minutes of that, and
said, 'I can't do this stuff.'"[70] Because, for much
of the film, Serpico is an outsider on the inside,
whose discomfort around other cops is palpable,
this experience might have been more useful than
Pacino implies. Still, he swiftly moved on, and
went straight to the source.

Since leaving the NYPD, Frank Serpico had
been living in Switzerland. He came to stay with
Pacino in a summer rental in Montauk, on New
York's Long Island. Pacino was already locked into
a contract to make the movie, with a Bregman-
negotiated deal that would give him a share of the
profits, but spending time with Serpico gave the
actor a personal connection to the material.
"The moment I shook his hand and looked into

his eyes," Pacino recalled, "I understood what that
movie could be."[71]

The biggest revelation came one night when,
as the pair sat gazing meditatively at the water,
Pacino broke the silence to ask Serpico why he
had fought so hard against the system. Serpico
answered, "If I didn't, who would I be when
I listened to a piece of music?" For an actor who
spoke of his own craft in musical terms, this was
a lightbulb moment. "I mean, what a way of
putting it!" Pacino exclaimed later. "That's the
kind of guy he was."[72]

The End of Idealism

We first see Pacino's Serpico immediately after
he's been shot in the line of duty. En route to the
hospital, his head thrown back and blood drip-
ping down his bearded cheek, his pose unavoid-
ably calls to mind Christ on the cross — the first
hint that Frank Serpico's story is a martyr's tale.
And before Serpico even arrives at the hospital,
Lumet cuts away to conversations among cops
that clue us in on the idea that our hero was
cut down by the animosity of his peers. Once
in the emergency room, perched vulnerably on
the brink between life and death, Frank flashes
back to his graduation from the police academy.
The film will essentially unfurl as a continuous
flashback, from Serpico's youthful, idealistic first
days in uniform, to his increasing frustration

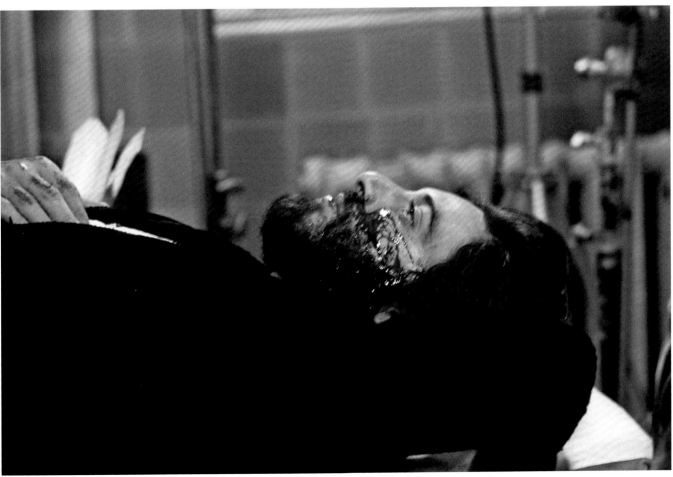

trying to enforce laws in a hopelessly fixed police department (and while wearing increasingly ironic undercover plainclothes getups), to the night of the shooting. In its aftermath, Serpico accepts defeat, preserving his dignity by walking away.

Seen through the eyes of Serpico—the first-generation son of Italian immigrant cobblers, who dreamed of being a cop since childhood—the corruption of the police department is not only blatant but absurd and insidious in its banality. At a deli, on a lunch break with another cop, Serpico finds he's forced to accept a free, sub-standard meal in exchange for overlooking the restaurant's parking violations, and is not allowed to pay out of pocket to get a decent sandwich. The rottenness is so endemic that it even extends to lunch. And it doesn't get better as Serpico moves up the ladder. Transferred to a new precinct, Serpico is handed an envelope of cash on his first day by another officer. He's advised to take it to "the most honest cop" around, who meets Serpico at an old-boys'-club restaurant and barely seems to listen as the young officer explains his concerns. "Don't you think it was kind of stupid to take an envelope from someone you didn't know?" the old-timer asks blithely, while squeezing a whole lemon on the lobster he's ordered for lunch.

The passage of time is charted by the length and mass of Pacino's facial hair (the picture was filmed in reverse sequence, so that the actor could start with a full beard and shed layers as

the production went along). *Serpico* at times feels like a slog, hammering home the same basic point over and over again—that, within this twisted system, Serpico is criminalized for trying to do the right thing—through eventually interchangeable scenes of our hero coolly interacting with bad cops (who constitute the majority of his colleagues) and venting his rage and frustration at his few confidants: Bob Blair (Tony Roberts) a proto-preppy whose political savvy complements Serpico's street smarts; the Catholic Captain McClain (Biff McGuire); and two girlfriends, ethereal dancer Leslie (Cornelia Sharpe) and earthy nurse Laurie (Barbara Eda-Young).

In dealing with the women in Serpico's life, the film falls into the rote biopic trap of using the protagonist's love interests as ciphers through which to define different facets of his own personality and his changing priorities. Both blond and similarly named, Laurie and Leslie are distinguished solely by the different functions they serve in terms of moving the narrative. Leslie brings Frank (who moves to Greenwich Village and starts calling himself "Paco" as he distances himself from the groupthink of the NYPD) into her bohemian world, where her artist friends are instantly distrustful when they find out he's a cop. Meanwhile, the literature and interest in dance Serpico picks up from Leslie gets him branded as a "weirdo" at work. Leslie then proves her own hypocrisy by leaving Frank to marry a wealthy

doctor. His subsequent relationship with Laurie, a healer by trade and maternal by nature, is a device to demonstrate Serpico's worsening obsession with fixing his damaged professional life, and his incremental alienation from personal relationships and the domestic sphere.

Broken down by the politics that are keeping the mayor from taking a stand against police corruption, Serpico explodes at his closest colleague, Blair, in plain view of Laurie. Blair storms off, and without missing a beat, in the same enraged tone of voice, Frank berates the girl for not tidying up their apartment: "Look, when I come home, I want a clean house!" His weary paramour responds, "Don't take it out on me, Frank." But his work struggles have become all-consuming. A few scenes later, he all but dares her to leave him if she can't support his struggle. Eventually, she does. Because he's become so jaded, when he does encounter someone, like Laurie, who shares his ideals, and who is not double-dealing him or asking him to compromise his ethics, he can't appreciate it. As much as *Serpico* is a portrait of a lone man going against the system, it's also a portrait of the day-to-day untenability of that position. If Pacino's performance in *The Godfather* is the finest film portrait ever of "the hardening of a heart,"[73] his performance in *Serpico* is, arguably, the era's definitive portrait of the death of idealism.

Roughly the first half of the movie constitutes the one-by-one wearing down of Serpico's nerves. It seems that the last one snaps during one of the film's central scenes in which Serpico makes a plainclothes arrest of a loan shark, only to discover the crook is known and liked by Serpico's fellow cops. Dressed as a filthy busboy — "I thought you were a junkie!" the perp laughs as he's taken into custody — Serpico throws an incredible, chair tossing tantrum in the police headquarters when he catches the other cops sitting around laughing with the crook, and, by extension, at him.

Once Serpico's last nerve is worn down, Pacino goes into whirling dervish mode. In the next scene — a clandestine meeting with McClain in a park — it's clear that Serpico's been pushed to the brink by the way he enters the scene, barking his frustrations at full volume. As the captain tries to explain that the department "washes its own laundry," Pacino raises his own volume, drowning out the other actor: "We do not wash our own laundry. It just gets DIRTIER!" Though both men are shown in a medium shot, and it's evident that the captain is quite a bit taller than Serpico, Pacino seems to tower over the other man through strength of his voice alone. These two scenes are definitive examples of how the Pacino crescendo works in concert with the narrative: as the character's power and/or control decreases, Pacino's performance gets bigger, louder, and more external.

If Pacino's performance could be measured on an audio-frequency meter, during the park scene the needle would hit the red. But that's as high as he goes in this movie. In subsequent scenes, Pacino shows Serpico's weariness, his increasing resignation to the futility of fighting for his ideals. With nothing left to lose, he openly defies and talks back to his superiors. When an investigation into corruption is mounted, Serpico can tell that it's a sham. "This is bullshit," he says. Pacino doesn't give the line the full-throttle rage of his confrontation with McClain. Instead, he simply has Serpico look the police power brokers straight in the eyes, and, barely raising his voice, announce clearly and unambiguously that he sees right through them. Here, through his performance style alone, Pacino makes the point that power doesn't have to be conferred from above, but is something a man can find within himself and use to dominate those whose institutional power is higher on paper.

Once Serpico is shot, he accepts that he's fought as far and as long as he can, and Pacino brings the performance down even further, to a register almost as minimalist as the young Michael Corleone. The comparison feels particularly apt in one of the film's final scenes, which has vague echoes of the scene in *The Godfather* in which Michael visits his father in the hospital after the attempt on Vito's life. Lying in the hospital, recovering from the shooting, Serpico is handed a gold detective badge, an honor that he had been fighting for, in vain, for much of the movie. As Serpico takes the miniature shield in his hand, the actor's eyes fill with tears, and he says, "What's this for? For being an honest cop? Or for being stupid enough to get shot in the face?" Mumbling as though speaking around the wound in Serpico's cheek, his voice almost whistling through his clenched teeth, Pacino's tone of voice resembles Brando's as Vito, crossed with the near-musical pitch of James Cagney—who, in his gangster films of the 1930s, was the archetypical Hollywood antihero, representing the wish-fulfillment fantasies of the oppressed and repressed American everyman.

The final shot of the movie is of Serpico sitting on a curb, in front of a steamer that he's apparently about to board, with a suitcase and his dog. We're not sure whether he even knows that he even knows where he's going, but we do know that he knows he can't stay where he is. On-screen titles confirm that while the real Serpico exiled himself to Europe, his battles fundamentally changed business as usual in the police force. In essence, Serpico sacrificed himself for the good of others—but once such idealism is lost, there's no going back. It's a heroic arc, and a spiritual tragedy, that would be repeated by the Pacino characters at the center of *Dog Day Afternoon* and *...And Justice for All*.

Becoming Al Pacino

Serpico was built around Pacino, and its massive box-office and critical success ensured that his star would only rise further as a result. But some critics suggested that the actor had yet to come into his own, criticizing Pacino simply for what they felt was an unshakable resemblance to Dustin Hoffman.[74] This was something Pacino had, of course, heard before, but *Serpico*'s success would allow Pacino to finally differentiate himself from Hoffman once and for all, an eventuality that some critics saw coming.

"Pacino has an unsettling resemblance to Dustin Hoffman, but he also has the ability to convey a genuine passion," noted Frank Rich in *New Times*. "Just watch his eyes: by the film's climax they become so hungry one knows that all the grand juries in the world will never satisfy him."[75] *New York*'s Judith Crist also noted that Pacino made any once-valid comparisons to Hoffman moot; she called his Serpico "one of the outstanding performances of the year."[76] Pacino himself had the final word on the matter in 1975: "They once asked me to understudy Dustin on Broadway, but I was busy. I love his work and think he's brilliant. But when we act, I think a whole different thing comes across. And, he *is* older—and shorter."[77]

If *The Godfather* had made Pacino a known quality, it was *Serpico* that put him in the power position as a top star. It was the first film in which he not only appeared on screen but also participated enthusiastically off screen, and it gave him new respect for acting for the camera. "With *Serpico* I was more on the inside," Pacino said. "I found out how to act a scene, what you do when you write a scene, what it's like to work together with people like Lumet, Marty Bregman and the editor Dede Allen."[78]

He was adamant to remain an actor—a profession he spoke of as though it were working-class—and not become a celebrity, and thus lose touch with the everymen he played. "There was a time when you didn't become an actor unless you loved to act. Actors today get to a certain point where they become affluent and cavort with kings and queens and oil barons and all the fashionable people... I don't cavort. I lead a simple, humble life. My lifestyle is pretty much the same as it's always been. I'm an actor."[79] There was honesty in that statement. As late as 1979, Pacino lived alone in a three-room Manhattan apartment, with only rudimentary furniture and appliances—the better to make room for his stacks of books, plays, and scripts.

Life in the Bottle

Nominated for his second Oscar for the part, Pacino attended the Academy Awards ceremony for the first time. "I was sitting in the third or fourth row with Diane Keaton," Pacino recalled a few years later. "Jeff Bridges was there with his girl. No one expected me to come. I was a little high... I sat there and tried to look indifferent because I was so nervous. Any time I'm nervous, I try to put on an indifferent or cold look. At one point I turned to Jeff Bridges and said, 'Hey, looks like there won't be time to get to the Best Actor awards.' He gave me a strange look. He said, 'Oh, really? It's three hours long.' I thought it was an hour TV show. Can you imagine that? And I had to pee—bad. So I popped a Valium. Actually, I was eating Valium like they were candy. Chewed on them. Finally came the Best Actor. Can you imagine the shape I was in?... I was praying, 'Please don't let it be me. Please.' And I hear... 'Jack Lemmon.' I was just so happy I didn't have to get up, because I never would have made it."[80]

It wasn't the first or last time that Pacino would sabotage himself with his compulsive intoxication. "Drinking and smoking grass were a part of my life as far back as I can remember," he said in 1979.[81] By the time he was in his early thirties and experiencing sudden fame, that part of his life was starting to become debilitating; he was, as he put it, "trying to get out of a barrel." One night during that period, after a three-day drinking binge, Pacino was taking a bath in the apartment he shared with his longtime girlfriend Jill Clayburgh. "And she came into the bathroom and sat down and said, 'I suddenly feel lonely. But you are drunk.' I was pickled. It was as though there was fog on my glasses. The windshield wipers weren't working."[82] Their five-year relationship ended soon afterward.

During the first few years of his screen stardom, Pacino was not only drinking heavily, he was all but bragging about it, presenting an image of himself as an actor whose hard play further legitimized his hard work. "Laurence Olivier was right when he said a drink after the show is the best thing about the theater," he told one interviewer in 1975. "But I never touch a drop when I'm working—and I've given up three-day binges. Coming out of them leaves me too depressed." Doing press apparently didn't count as "working." In yet another interview, he revealed that the black walking stick he kept by his side had a false top—he unscrewed it to reveal a narrow flask full of booze.[83]

"I don't think you'll be seeing me in too many movies," he said in 1973, in an interview that took place over multiple vodkas in a New York bar. "I still want to play Hamlet, and time's running out." Pacino paused. "Ah hell...who wants to play Hamlet? I just want to go home to bed."[84] He has frequently discussed his use of alcohol as a crutch to help deal with the initial onslaught of fame. As he recalled in 1985, "There was a lot of stimuli around, and the more sensitive you are, the more you think you need to dull your senses with drugs or alcohol. Slowly you realize what you could become if you stopped. I stopped slowly. And things got a little clearer. But I mean just a *little*..."[85]

→ Comparison of Script Dialogue to Shot Dialogue to Show Improvisation

Scene 160, from an unpublished Serpico *script, dated June 18, 1973. Accessed at Academy of Motion Picture Arts and Sciences' Margaret Herrick Library, pages 89–90.*

CAPTAIN McCLAIN
Hello, Frank. How have you been, Frank? It's been a long time…

FRANK SERPICO
Yes. It has. Captain, I've had it. I'm up to here with the filth up there. I can't take it. I have to get out. If I have to go back in uniform, that's fine with me. I can't wait anymore for Delaney to call. I can't play their games anymore…

CAPTAIN McCLAIN
Frank, I had no idea. You mean you never heard from the commissioner?

FRANK SERPICO
Not a peep. No, sir. Directly or indirectly. No sign of any kind of undercover investigation. Nothing.

CAPTAIN McCLAIN
I didn't know.

FRANK SERPICO
Captain, I think it's only fair to tell you, I've been to outside agencies.

CAPTAIN McCLAIN
(*suddenly alert*)
What outside agencies?

FRANK SERPICO
Well, I don't know, I don't really think I should discuss it with you…

CAPTAIN McCLAIN
You can get into trouble for that, Frank. We wash our own laundry.

FRANK SERPICO
I always thought so. But the reality is, we don't. It just gets dirtier. I'm not holding back anymore. I don't care who

gets it, including myself. I've been to outside agencies and I'll go to more if I have to…

CAPTAIN McCLAIN
Let me see what I can do.

Actual dialogue from finished film, transcribed:

CAPTAIN McCLAIN
It's good to see you again, Frank.

FRANK SERPICO
That's it. I've had it. I'm finished.

CAPTAIN McCLAIN
What's wrong?

FRANK SERPICO
I can't take it anymore. I gotta get out. If I have to go back to uniform, I'm going back to uniform. I can't wait for Delaney to call, and I can't play their game anymore. I'm right in the middle. I can't take it.

CAPTAIN McCLAIN
You mean to say the commissioner didn't get in touch with you?

FRANK SERPICO
No, he didn't get in touch with me. Not a word, no investigation, no undercover work, nothing.

CAPTAIN McCLAIN
(*talking over Serpico*)
I had no idea.

FRANK SERPICO
Well. Captain, I think it's only fair to tell you, I've been to outside agencies. I'm gonna go to more if I have to.

CAPTAIN McCLAIN
What outside agencies? Holy mother of God! Frank, we wash our own laundry around here!

FRANK SERPICO
Oh, yeah?

CAPTAIN McCLAIN
Now, you could be brought up on charges for this.

FRANK SERPICO
(*talking over McClain*)
I always thought so, but the reality is, we do not wash our own laundry. It just gets dirtier!

CAPTAIN McCLAIN
You are in trouble!

FRANK SERPICO
I don't care if I'm in trouble. I don't care who gets it anymore, including myself. Because if I have to go to outside agencies —

CAPTAIN McCLAIN
You stay away from outside agencies.

FRANK SERPICO
Where am I gonna go?

CAPTAIN McCLAIN
You hear me, Serpico, stay away from outside agencies.

FRANK SERPICO
WHERE AM I GONNA GO?

CAPTAIN McCLAIN
You just wait until you hear from me!

FRANK SERPICO
I've been waiting for a year and a half!

CAPTAIN McCLAIN
I'll be in touch with you, Frank. (*Captain McClain starts walking away*)

FRANK SERPICO
That's not enough! (*pause*) Where am I gonna go?

FRANK SERPICO
(*shouting at Captain McClain's back*)
It's my life, you fuck!

4

Sonny Wortzik

Dog Day Afternoon (1975)
Sidney Lumet

"When I made those films, I wasn't allowed to make a normal picture. Every picture I made had to have this thing in it. There was a kind of unconscious pressure I felt."
—Al Pacino, 2004[86]

The item that ran in the January 17, 1973, edition of *Variety* was headlined, GAY BANK ROBBER TO BE FILM HERO. The news: producer Martin Elfand had paid $7,500 for the life rights of John Wojtowicz, a young man who had held up a Brooklyn bank the previous summer. During the ensuing standoff with police, Wojtowicz had admitted that although he was legally married to the mother of his two children, he later had a ceremony to marry a man named Ernest Aron. The bank robbery was an attempt to procure cash so that Aron—who self-identified as a transsexual woman named Liz Eden—could have a sex-change operation. The *Variety* story reported that Wojtowicz was giving a third of his life-rights paycheck to Aron/Eden for that very reason.

The as-yet-untitled movie, it was reported, was to be produced by Elfand and scripted by Thomas Moore and P. F. Kluge, authors of a *LIFE* magazine exposé on Wojtowicz, with Randy Wicker, then a correspondent for the gay herald *The Advocate*, serving as "script consultant." In the end, none of the above would be credited as participants on *Dog Day Afternoon*, the film Sidney Lumet was to make, inspired by the Wojtowicz incident. One anecdote in the *Variety* item indicated the direction the fledging movie was headed: "Director and cast have not been set, but Wicker reports showing a videotape of the 'marriage' between Wojtowicz and Aron to Al Pacino who bears a striking resemblance to Wojtowicz. Pic's emphasis is expected to be less on the gay subculture than on the robbery derring-do."

Lumet's film did skirt some thornier aspects of its antihero's sexual identity—including the real-life inspiration's firm separation from his female wife that preceded his marriage to Aron; his participation in the Gay Activists Alliance; and the highly cinematic theory, as reported at length by the *Village Voice*,[87] that Wojtowicz and his accomplices had acted on order of the Gambino crime family, who ran a number of Greenwich Village gay bars, and whose role within the Five Families of the Mafia had helped

to inspire *The Godfather*. Wojtowicz himself would write a lengthy letter of complaint about the film to the *New York Times* (who refused to publish it), claiming "the movie to be only 30 percent true... All through the movie they take facts that were true but then present them differently." Wojtowicz would lay the blame for the neutering of his story on "the screen writer, Mr. Frank Pierson, for not going into a more explanatory and deeper characterization of the people involved. But Hollywood wants to make money, and if sacrificing the truth or exploiting the lives of real people is the way to make money, then that's what they do."[88] *Dog Day Afternoon* may not present Wojtowicz's reality to the letter, but given the period and circumstances of its production, it's a fairly radical work, concerned with "reality" in ways that were both daringly topical at the time of its release and prescient, particularly in regards to its depiction of stardom in an always-on media age.

After *Serpico*, Pacino's second collaboration with Lumet gave the actor another opportunity to serve as kind of a mouthpiece for the angst of the American male in a period of transition. But while in *Serpico* the Pacino character's steadfast morality was the reason given for his inability to assimilate, in *Dog Day Afternoon* the Pacino character's morality was bound up in a different kind of otherness: specifically, his bisexuality, and generally, his inability to reconcile the contradictions of his nature. This kind of inquiry into the divided self, present as at least a subtextual notion from the very beginning in Pacino's chosen characters, was now more than subtext: it was the subject of the movie.

The Actor as Auteur

By June 1974, when Pacino's casting in *Dog Day Afternoon* was publicly confirmed, the actor was a bigger star than ever. He had been nominated for two consecutive Oscars, for *The Godfather* and *Serpico*. *The Godfather Part II* was in the can, awaiting a highly anticipated Christmas 1974 release. *Serpico*'s box-office gross was a then-stellar $25 million and counting—a fact Warner Bros. trumpeted in their press release announcing that *Dog Day* would reunite star Pacino and director Sidney Lumet. Shooting began in

Al Pacino as Sonny Wortzik in Sidney Lumet's *Dog Day Afternoon* (1975).

63

September 1974 and was finished by the end of November—two weeks ahead of schedule—despite a troubled beginning.

As a heterosexual sex symbol, playing a man in a romantic relationship with another man was something Pacino wasn't completely comfortable with. According to screenwriter Frank Pierson, halfway through the rehearsal period, Pacino was on the verge of quitting the picture. "Al said it had become apparent in the course of the rehearsals that the homosexuality of the relationship was the dominant thing, and he'd decided he didn't want to do that, for a lot of reasons, personal and professional," Pierson remembered.

In Pierson's script, there had been a kiss between Pacino's character and his "male wife," played by Chris Sarandon. "Al said he would not do that scene," Pierson continued. "What it got down to was, Al said, 'I want to take out all the references to sex—all that has to go. Furthermore, I won't appear in a scene where I have to be face-to-face with him.' So I said, 'The only way you'll play a scene together is on the telephone?' And he said, 'That's right.' So I said, 'I don't see anything else to do now but send the screenplay to Dustin Hoffman.' And Al said, 'Before you do that, I wish you'd just think of one thing: You've had marriages, and you've had love affairs in which there have been climactic scenes, the end of love, the saying goodbye. And in how many of those real-life situations has sex ever come into

it, in terms of what you said to each other? Why can't you write a relationship about two people who love each other and can't find a way to live with each other?' And I saw instantly that he was absolutely, totally right! And I said, 'You sonovabitch, why didn't you think of this four months ago, when there was some time to write this?'" [89]

Even after that problem was solved, after watching the first dailies, Pacino insisted that they reshoot. "I thought, *This is incredible. There's* nobody *up there*." Pacino proclaimed. "I came home, got a bottle of wine, and stayed up all night because I had neglected to work on certain things, and it was very important for me to see that day's rushes, because there wasn't a character." [90] These anecdotes offer evidence that, once again, Pacino was exercising a level of control over the authorship of the film that could be considered extraordinary for "just" an actor.

More Than Meets the Eye

Dog Day Afternoon begins with a montage of establishing shots: a dog roots through trash, anonymous bodies crowd a beach and a public pool, construction work drones on—it's summer in New York. A movie theater marquee advertises *A Star Is Born*—an early clue that the real subject of the movie will be the changing face of media and the power of an audience's gaze.

Sidney Lumet on Directing Al Pacino

"One of the most difficult acting scenes I've ever encountered was on *Dog Day Afternoon.* About two-thirds of the way through the movie, Pacino makes two phone calls: one to his 'wife' and lover, who's at a barbershop across the street, and the second to his 'real' wife, in her home.

"I knew Al would build up the fullest head of steam if we could do it in one take. The scene took place at night. The character had been in the bank for twelve hours. He had to seem spent, exhausted. When we're that tired, emotions flow more easily. And that's what I wanted.

"[...] I wanted Al's concentration at its peak. I cleared the set and then, about five feet behind the camera, put up blackflats so that even the rest of the physical set was blocked out. The propman had rigged the phones so the off-camera actors could speak into phones across the street and Al would really hear them on his phone.

"One of the best ways of accumulating emotion is to go as rapidly as possible from one take to the next. The actor begins the second take on the emotional level he reached at the end of the first take. Sometimes I don't even cut the camera. I'll say quietly, 'Don't cut the camera—everybody back to their opening positions and we're going again. OK, from the top: Action!' [...]

"I knew a second take would mean a serious interruption for Al. We'd have to reload one of the cameras... The whole process, done at top speed, takes two or three minutes, enough time for Al to cool off. So I put up a black tent to block off both cameras and the men operating them. We cut two holes for the lenses. And I had the second assistant cameramen (there are three men on a camera crew: operator, focus puller, and second assistant) hold an extra film magazine in his lap, in case we needed it.

"We rolled... The take ended. It was wonderful. But something told me to go again... I called out gently, 'Al, back to the top, I want to go again.' He looked at me as if I'd gone mad. He'd gone full out and was exhausted. He said, 'What?! You're kidding!' I said, 'Al, we have to. Roll camera.'

"[...] By the end of the second take, Al didn't know where he was anymore. He finished his lines, and, in sheer exhaustion, looked around helplessly. Then, by accident, he looked directly at me. Tears were rolling down my face because he'd moved me so. His eyes locked into mine and he burst into tears, then slumped over the desk he'd been sitting at. I called, 'Cut! Print!' and leapt into the air. That take is some of the best film acting I've ever seen."[h]

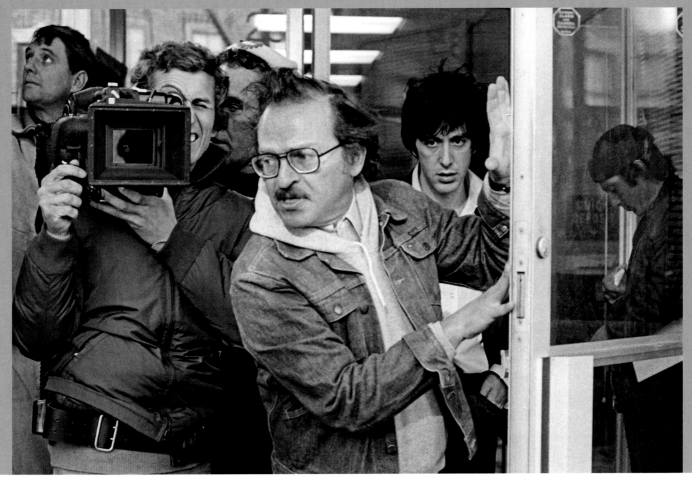

The story takes place in what is essentially a single location—the bank and the area immediately surrounding it—but that space is functionally stratified in ways that call to mind the constructs of both stage and screen performance. If the sidewalk in front of the bank is Sonny's stage, in front of which the audience gathers to cheer him on, the bank itself is backstage, where Sonny works out his performance. However, the police occupation of the storefront across the street—separated from Sonny by his "fans"— adds another layer, one that takes the events out of the context of stage acting and into the context of screen acting. Once the FBI start manipulating the situation from a distance—"directing" the scene, whether Sonny, the star, realizes it or not—*Dog Day Afternoon* becomes a clear presage of contemporary "reality" TV.

Lumet and Pierson don't reveal Sonny's sexual identity to viewers until quite a ways into the film, but the character's outsider status, his inadequacy as a bank robber, and his oddness as a man is evident right from the beginning. As Sonny and his partner, Sal (John Cazale), enter the bank, Pacino's wide eyes unmistakably convey nervousness. Once the operation begins, he gets tangled up in his gun, and tries to cover the security camera but because he's too short to reach it, he jumps and flails. In his mid-thirties, Pacino uses his body to convey youthful inexperience and energy. Swift and spry, he seems to be constantly moving, virtually bouncing across and between the film's "stages." Lumet's handheld camera follows him as he slides across the bank's waxed floor.

Class and sex conflicts are evident within the bank. The workers consist primarily of women employed by a white male. The man instructs his female staff to cooperate with the criminals in their midst. One of the lady employees asks the profane Sonny to watch his language, appealing to an old-fashioned sense of etiquette regarding how men should behave around women. He responds, "I speak what I feel, you know?" Not only is Sonny of the wrong kind of upbringing to value such superficial distinctions regarding mixed company, but he also makes it clear that his version of manhood is to follow his feelings, regardless of its effect on the women around him.

But it's that vulnerability, the priority he gives to his "feelings" over rationality, that sinks him as a bank robber. The ladies of the bank see right through him. "Do you even have a plan?" asks one accusatorially. "I know a lot about a lot of things," he responds—and Pacino underlines the bravado of the claim, giving the audience the impression that the opposite is true. And yet, shortly thereafter, he announces that his plan is to confront the cops with a carefully chosen shield. "I'll take one of the girls, a married one with kids. Cops don't like it in the papers when they shoot a married woman with kids." This calculation, reflecting an

understanding of how fear of the way the media works can have an impact on the enforcement of the law, suggests that Sonny might know more than he lets on.

That suggestion is amplified when Sonny claims that he and his partner Sal are "Vietnam veterans, so killing don't mean anything to us." Again, Pacino gives the line ironic meaning with his reading. We know that killing would mean something to Sonny, because he's already told the people in the bank that, because he's Catholic, he doesn't want to hurt them. At the same time, that this is what he tells the police suggests he understands the sociopolitical climate well enough to know that "Vietnam veteran" is a hot potato of a phrase that has the power to change the tenor of the confrontation. Pacino spits out this line with a blasé deadpan that simultaneously reinforces the disaffection he's trying to sell to the cops, while clueing the audience in on the misdirection.

Attica!

Perhaps more than any other serious American actor of the last half of the twentieth century, Al Pacino is associated with catchphrases popularized by his films—"Say hello to my little friend!" from *Scarface*; "Just when I think I'm out, they pull me back in!" from *The Godfather Part III*. It's a trend that began with *Dog Day*

Afternoon, with Sonny rising up against an unfair system with his cry, "Attica! Attica!"

In 1971, approximately half of the population at Attica Correctional Facility in New York instigated an organized riot in protest of overcrowding in the prison. The inmates held dozens of prison staff hostage for four days, and negotiations ended with Governor Nelson Rockefeller calling in the state police to use deadly force. Thirty-nine people died. In the summer of 1972, when the events dramatized in *Dog Day Afternoon* took place, the Attica incident was fresh in the public consciousness, as an example of an abusive use of institutional power.

Sonny uses the memory of Attica to galvanize the crowd that gathers to watch his standoff with the police unfold. When the assembled mob cheers in response to his chant, he feeds off their energy, preening and strutting for the crowd. Their attention transforms Sonny from a twitchy ball of nervous incompetence into a powerful conductor of a public spectacle. On the street and inside the bank, he seems like two different people.

The "Attica!" cry is key to the film, and to Pacino's performance within it. Pacino's most fundamental connection to the character came from their shared experience of class, of what it meant to be born into nothing and to reach, against all odds, for something extraordinary. "Al understands these people. He grew up in a very rough neighborhood and survived," Marty

Bregman said. "Al is a street guy."[91] In *Serpico*, Pacino played a cop who goes against a corrupt system, thus representing the everyman who is exploited and oppressed by that system. In *Dog Day Afternoon*, he fuses that notion of the everyman with the theme of public burlesque as resistance against the straight life found in *Scarecrow*. If *Serpico* established Pacino as an icon whose voice spoke for the people and against the status quo, with "Attica!" the actor was given a slogan that reduced that everyman symbolism to a repeatable shorthand.

The scene is also where, to quote that earlier-glimpsed theater marquee, a star is born. For Pacino, the film was clearly about the way widespread acknowledgment of the function and possibilities of the media was changing human behavior. "When the delivery boy delivers the pizza and then turns around to the crowd and says, in effect, 'I'm a star!' It hit right where we're at—the kind of energy wrapped up in the media and with imagery and fantasy and film," he said. "We don't know enough about media yet, we don't know its effect on us. It's new. It's got to do something to us."[92]

Improvised Solutions

The first time Al Pacino played a character based on a living person in a Sidney Lumet film—Frank Serpico in *Serpico*—the actor relied heavily on the time he spent with the inspiration for the character. Not so the second time. Years after the fact, Pacino admitted that he had "avoided meeting" John Wojtowicz, the basis for Sonny in *Dog Day Afternoon*. "That was a mistake," he conceded. "It would have served me to meet him. It always does."[93]

Working without referencing the primary source, Pacino built his character the Actors Studio way. While Pacino had ad-libbed some lines on *Serpico*, on *Dog Day* Lumet allowed his actors the freedom to go off script entirely. Lumet estimated that 60 percent of the dialogue was improvised. "One of the actors asked if they could use their own words when they wanted to," Lumet wrote in his memoir, *Making Movies*. "For the first time in my career, I said, 'Yes.'"[94] While they followed the structure of Pierson's Oscar-winning screenplay, within that structure, improvising the actual spoken language fit with Pacino's version of the Method, his process of becoming another person by drawing on his own personal thoughts, feelings, and experiences.

Improvisation was how Pacino solved problems—like the problem of expressing his character's love for another man. In place of the Pierson-scripted kiss that was nixed, Pacino and Lumet sought to create an equivalent or even greater intensity of feeling without physical contact. In the script, Sonny demands to see Leon (Chris Sarandon), his male wife, who is pulled out

of a mental ward and brought to the scene of the crime. But in the filmed version, Leon refuses to cross the street from the makeshift police headquarters to see Sonny face-to-face at the bank. Instead, the two talk on the phone, with Leon essentially breaking up with Sonny, and Sonny coming to the heartbreaking realization that the love he thought had justified his criminal actions is over, and he's out of options. "The entire phone call was an improvisation that was written by Sidney Lumet, myself and Chris Sarandon," Pacino said. "We spent days improvising, and it was transcribed, and that was turned into a scene."[95]

The Failure of the Everyman

At age thirty-five, Pacino still has a youthful beauty in *Dog Day Afternoon*, but we can detect the first signs of age: bags are starting to form under his eyes, and even before the character's struggle against the dominant order ends in failure, Pacino's face broadcasts a sense of fatigue, and you get the sense that it's cumulative. *Dog Day*'s vision of the futility of resistance builds on *Serpico*'s. Men like Sonny and Frank are noble, charismatic, sexy, but also outnumbered, impotent, doomed. At the end of the film, when Sonny watches his partner Sal die and submits to his own fate, Pacino's eyes—which, in previous scenes, darted frantically as his body bounced across the "stage" in front of the bank—appear

fully glazed over, any youthful idealism completely dissipated.

Call it a coming of age. Pacino would bring with him that acquired wisdom, and the weariness that goes with it, into the final film in the actor's arc as the everyman fighting in vain against an increasingly corrupt world, *...And Justice for All*.

5

Arthur Kirkland

...And Justice for All (1979)
Norman Jewison

"I have never seen a film like this before. It has certain exaggerations, but it gets real... and yet not real."[96]
—Al Pacino, 1979

Pacino had become a star within a wave of American cinema that put a premium on the real. Filmmakers like Francis Ford Coppola, Jerry Schatzberg, and Sidney Lumet had been influenced by French and Italian cinema of the late 1950s and 1960s, which made use of some of the aesthetics and the portable equipment associated with documentary to tell stories of everyday lives. And with the success of *Easy Rider*—a low-budget road movie with naturalistic dialogue and performances—commercial Hollywood embraced films made by young directors who sought to tell stories about "real lives" using filmmaking techniques, from camerawork to dialogue to performance style, that represented a fresh, more lifelike alternative to classical film artifice.

That wave wouldn't last, of course. Arguably, *The Godfather*—whose director, Coppola, had a neorealist impulse and fought to bring some element of authenticity to the production—was instrumental in the move away from the real, as its blockbuster success launched the modern notion of the film franchise. By the end of the 1970s, with the rise of movies like *Star Wars* and *Jaws*, the studio system that had been so crippled in the 1960s that it was willing to try anything was regrouping behind event films, and the American film industry would become increasingly corporate in the next decade. By the 1980s, the "real" would have fallen out of fashion.

Al Pacino's final film of the 1970s, *...And Justice for All*, constitutes a crucial point of transition. It is, as Pacino noted, both real... and yet not real. As such, it effectively closes the door on Pacino's persona of the 1970s, and opens the door to the next phase of his career, the one embodied by the distinctly larger-than-life *Scarface*.

Funny Ha Ha?

Directed by Norman Jewison from a script by Barry Levinson and Valerie Curtin, *...And Justice for All* takes its title from the Pledge of Allegiance, the oath to the American flag as an embodiment of "one nation under God, indivisible, with liberty and justice for all." These words, recited before every session of Congress and by many American public school kids at the start of their school day, constitute probably the most succinct, familiar summation of what America is supposed to stand for. The sound of children reciting the Pledge is heard over the film's opening credits, confirming that the title's appropriation of the phrase is both ironic (there is *not* justice for all) and earnest, a willfully naïve reminder of the way things ought to be.

Baltimore public defense attorney Arthur Kirkland (Pacino) is a recently divorced workaholic whose only close personal relationship is with his senile grandfather (Lee Strasberg), who no longer seems to recognize that his grandson is a lawyer. Over the course of the film, Arthur juggles three cases. He defends a black transvestite on a soliciting charge; he struggles to free a white working-class man who wrongly spent two years in jail in a case of mistaken identity; and he's blackmailed into representing the powerful Judge Fleming (John Forsythe), whom Arthur despises, when he's accused of raping and beating a woman. Meanwhile, Arthur's partner Jay Porter (Jeffrey Tambor) goes into an emotional tailspin after discovering that a client he helped free was in fact a brutal murderer, and Arthur starts dating Gail (Christine Lahti), a lawyer he meets while giving a deposition to the ethics panel she chairs. Arthur eventually figures out that Gail is investigating him at the behest of the judge, who, it emerges, is not only guilty of rape but proud of it. Knowing that the judge will have him disbarred if he refuses to lead his defense, Arthur is nonetheless unable to make that ethical compromise.

The final scene of the film begins at the launch of Fleming's trial. Arthur starts to give a conventional opening statement, directed at poking holes in the prosecution's case. Then, as if out of the blue, he reveals that he knows Fleming is guilty. "Ladies and gentlemen of the jury, the prosecution is not going to get [my client] today, no—because I'm gonna get him! My client, the Honorable Henry T. Fleming, should go right to fucking jail! The son of a bitch is guilty!" The room explodes. The judge presiding over the trial bangs his gavel, telling Arthur he's out of order. "You're out of order!" Arthur shouts back, setting up what would become another great Pacino

Al Pacino as Arthur Kirkland in Norman Jewison's *...And Justice for All* (1979).

79

catchphrase. "You're out of order! The whole trial is out of order!" Talk about crescendos; from beginning to end, the scene and Pacino's performance in it arcs from piano to sforzando.

Arthur is ejected from the courtroom. His law career is almost certainly over. Sitting on the steps of the courthouse, he sees Jay marching back to work, his crisis apparently behind him. As he passes Arthur, Jay removes and replaces his toupee, as if tipping his hat. The film ends on a freeze-frame of Arthur—at the end of his rope, the future completely uncertain—his face frozen in a confused half smile. The credits roll to the film's theme song, a funk-pop tune by Dave Grusin and Alan and Marilyn Bergman called "Something Funny's Goin' On." The song's title could double as the movie's title, with "funny" alternately connoting comedy and something not quite right. Pacino had already made a name for himself in films that explored dualism. ...*And Justice for All* was more than two-faced—it was, by design, all over the place.

King Arthur in Baltimore?

Co-screenwriter Barry Levinson consciously modeled the story on the legend of King Arthur. Pacino's character, Arthur Kirkland, seeks to restore the lost dignity in a fallen Camelot— in this case, Baltimore, a key site in the American Revolution and one of the main metropolises during the early years of the United States. Arthur's Merlin is his grandfather, played by Pacino's own mentor, Lee Strasberg. Like King Arthur, this Arthur is betrayed by his lover— in this case, not Guinevere but Gail, a fellow lawyer whose ethics committee fingers Arthur for investigation, thus forcing him to take a case that will make him choose between selling out his own ethics or destroying his career.

But the clearly allegorical, Arthurian strain running through Levinson's screenplay clashes with director Jewison's interest in realism. The filmmaker built the production around real locations, and cast actual court workers, including real judges, as extras. "The idea began with the Russian director Pudovkin. He wrote a great deal about the believability of people in movies. He said that a policeman, fireman, postman, steel worker, anyone—doing his job—will be more convincing than even the finest actor." And however heightened the film's situations might be, the director was insistent that it was inspired by a real sense of disillusionment. "There was a time when the legal profession was inviolate," Jewison said. "Then came Watergate, and we began to wonder, 'How could all these lawyers with such high moral and ethical standards do such terrible things?' We're starting to realize that being in the law doesn't mean being above the law. And maybe that's the first step toward restoring our faith in the system."[97]

Justice has not ascended to the same status of undeniable classic as *Serpico* or *Dog Day Afternoon*, perhaps because of its divided nature, but the film's multiple-personality disorder is the perfect platform for a quintessentially dualistic Pacino character. The film's two conflicting impulses—realism and myth—are united in a lead performance that elevates the everyman into a larger-than-life hero.

Jewison referred to the film as a "terrifying comedy," noting that "it's an unusual role for Al Pacino. In past films, like *Dog Day Afternoon* and even *Serpico*, he's been the eccentric, cut off from a sane world. This time, he's the most rational person in the picture. It's everyone around him, and his environment, which is bizarre."[98] But Arthur's rationality and steadfast morality does make him an eccentric in this truly bizarre environment, which is the real world of an American urban justice system in the late 1970s, blown out of proportion and distorted into a funhouse mirror version of reality. As Levinson put it, the character was "a guy who's trying to practice his profession honestly and responsibly, without getting disbarred. Which is itself crazy."[99]

Cowriter Valerie Curtin noted that Pacino was ideal for the part because he "projects reality, unlike some actors who always seem larger than life"[100]—an interesting note, given the direction Pacino's performance style would go in subsequent years. In fact, his performance in *...And Justice for All* connects the seemingly opposite poles. When he explodes in rage against the machine—revealing the justice system to be the sham that it is with his outburst in the final scene—he is projecting reality through larger-than-life behavior, giving a drama that could only happen in the movies a grounding in emotional realism.

It's a risky film, and in fact, Pacino has spoken of taking on the project as though it was a grand experiment. When director Norman Jewison approached Pacino with the script, the actor asked him to "get some actors together" so that he could do a read through. "We read it aloud, and after I finished, it wasn't halfway bad. I thought it had a nice structure to it. I thought, if this thing works, what will make it work is that there are so many stories they're juggling," Pacino said. "It's a difficult film because it is so verbal; you really have to pay attention to it."[101]

Madness to His Method

"I worked with lawyers before filming began, so I felt kind of close to the courts," Pacino remembered shortly after finishing the film. "At one point recently a friend said to me he was having trouble with a contract, and I just instinctively said, 'Let me see that.' You get that feeling you are able to do these things. It's crazy. I literally took it from him and said, 'Well, maybe I can help you with this.' Can you imagine that? And I looked at the thing and I thought, What am I doing?"[102]

Jewison later related that he allowed for "a certain amount of improvisation" on the film. "Because Pacino is very creative, and we often take a scene we perhaps feel is a little bald character wise and try to work with it for two or three hours before we shoot it. We had a great experience on this film because Al, being a stage actor, did two weeks rehearsal before, which was wonderful for all of us because it doesn't happen too often. We did provide for it in the budget."[103]

The groundwork laid, the actor became indivisible from the character. "For almost 18 weeks, Al Pacino was Arthur Kirkland," Jewison marveled. "Even at night, when we'd finished shooting, he'd answer to that name. I remember sitting between Pacino and Strasberg at dinner. They were still so much into their roles that I found myself saying, 'Grandpa, pass the salt,' or 'Let's make it an early night, Arthur.'"[104]

Perhaps because he was so deep into character, Pacino refused to talk to journalists who visited the set. His mentor excused this apparently closed-off attitude as a sign of Pacino's passion. "Many people confuse his commitment to his work with temperament," Lee Strasberg said. "If anything, Al works too hard, which takes the energy out of him."[105]

In this case, Pacino's authorial instincts caused problems. In his autobiography, Jewison recalls clashing with Pacino on set; the actor had his own idea about the way his role should be played and the scenes staged. Fed up after a few contentious takes on one scene, Jewison walked off set and went and sat down outside. When Pacino asked what was going on, he was told that the director had gone home. Pacino went outside and sat down next to Jewison, who said, "Look, you see it one way and I see it another way. You might as well direct the picture, I'll go home." According to Jewison, after a moment's contemplation, Pacino gave in and agreed to go back on set and do it Jewison's way. "He didn't want to be known as a difficult guy to work with," Jewison continued, before writing, perhaps with a twinge of irony, that Pacino "could portray anger better than anyone I had ever worked with."[106]

Pacino's comments about Jewison were equally diplomatic, and offered just as much opportunity for reading between the lines. "He was different from anybody I had worked with before. The thing I like most about Norman is you get a sense of his involvement; he's constantly with the movie. He broods about it. Even after it's over, he's with the picture—he cares about it a great, great deal."[107]

The Last Angry Man

Justice has been described as "Serpico Takes On the Courts," and Pacino concurred that the

Lee Strasberg, seen here in the role of Grandpa Sam, had a special relationship with Al Pacino both on and off screen.

Following pages: Jeff McCullaugh (Thomas G. Waites), a client who was wrongly sentenced, talks to Kirkland.

It was 1973, and for the first time in Al Pacino's life, the thirty-three-year-old actor had all the power. Paramount needed him to agree to star in *The Godfather Part II*, and they were open to negotiation. So Pacino suggested that Lee Strasberg—longtime Actors Studio teacher and Pacino's personal friend—be given the role of Hyman Roth, the aged Jewish gangster with whom Michael enters into messy business. It was, incredibly, the seventy-two-year-old's first significant film role. Strasberg joked that he didn't need convincing: "How can a teacher refuse his student!"[i] Strasberg would be nominated for an Oscar for the role—his sole nod from the Academy in a lifetime dedicated to advancing the art of acting and the techniques known as the Method. Born in Poland in 1901, Strasberg emigrated with his family to the United States

when he was seven. He began acting in the 1920s, studying in New York with Stanislavski disciple Richard Boleslavsky. In 1929, Strasberg retired from stage performance to concentrate on teaching, founding the Group Theatre in 1931 and later joining, and eventually becoming synonymous with, the Actors Studio. Pacino and Strasberg's relationship went beyond teacher and student; starting with their meeting in the late 1960s and continuing until Strasberg's death, they enjoyed a close bond, with Pacino a regular dinner guest at the Strasberg home. A huge baseball fan, Pacino had an annual date to watch the World Series at the Strasberg residence. "We have this club," Strasberg noted. "It has a very exclusive membership—the kids and Al and myself. We sit and eat junk food and do a lot of cheering. No one else is allowed in."[j]

Pacino has continued to give credit to Strasberg for much of his career, but as close as they were, the student has not always followed Strasberg's teachings to the letter. Strasberg would again appear opposite his protégé in 1979, playing Pacino's character's grandfather in *...And Justice for All*. Strasberg became frustrated with Pacino's process on set, which often entailed going off script, improvising what he thought he would say in a given scene if he were in the character's situation. At one point, Strasberg heckled Pacino mid-ad-lib: "Al, learn your lines, dollink!"[k] Strasberg died suddenly in 1982, at the age of eighty-two. "It was so unexpected," Pacino told the *New York Times*. "What stood out was how youthful he was. He never seemed as old as his years. He was an inspiration."[l]

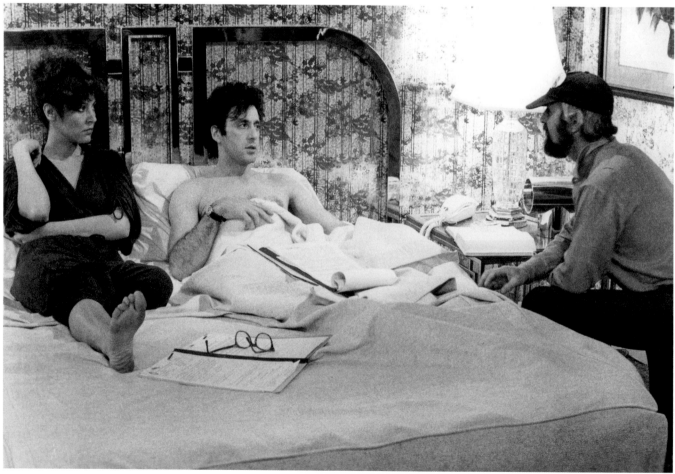

Opposite, top and bottom:
director Norman Jewison,
Al Pacino, and Christine Lahti
(playing Gail Packer) on the
set of ...And Justice for All.

The crew on the set of ...And
Justice for All.

similarities between the films are valid. "Although," he noted, "I find this character, Arthur Kirkland, to be less detached... I like him because of his involvement and his desire to be part of the system. He liked his work. Only the system drives him nuts." He continued, wondering aloud: "Does the audience have a sense of that? I hope they do. That the guy is giving it all up. You are seeing this guy struggle; it's the last time he's going to be up there. What he's trying to do is expose the system."[108]

The audience does, indeed, get the sense that Arthur is trying in good faith to play the game, but the rules keep changing. There's no question that *Justice* represents the third chapter in Pacino's mid-1970s trilogy of films, after *Serpico* and *Dog Day Afternoon*, in which one man, representing The People, goes up against urban law and order—The Man—and fails, his best intentions easily squashed by a system with no respect or use for the individual. But from start to finish, *Justice* travels a different path.

Arthur is first seen behind bars. Jailed for contempt of court (he threw a punch at Judge Fleming), Arthur is visibly exhausted and world-weary. This image puts the character in a league with Serpico and Sonny from *Dog Day*, in that all three are to be read as heroes whose heroism derives in part from their deviance. They have to bend or break the rules in order to do what they feel is the right thing, and they're treated like criminals because of it.

Still, there's a crucial difference between Kirkland and Pacino's two previous lone warriors against the system. Serpico and Sonny started out believing that they could take on their respective opponents and win, and only through the course of the film did they become aware of their own impotence. In *...And Justice for All*, the toll of battle is visible on Pacino's face from that very first scene at the jail. When we meet him, Arthur is still fighting, but he's much further along on the journey than the previous characters, much closer to giving up. It's almost as if Pacino has brought the lessons learned by Serpico and Sonny into the performance.

Like *Serpico*, Pacino's character in *Justice* seems to be the only man left in his world with a clear sense of right and wrong, a knowledge of "the way things are supposed to be" that the men around him have long since abandoned. Pacino portrays the burden of Arthur's responsibility by focusing on the fatigue of the never-ending fight. His eyes all but spin in their sockets; his tone of voice is even and direct, as if sheer exhaustion has worn down the character's social graces to the point where he's become physically incapable of saying anything other than exactly what he means.

The tone of the film flits between gritty "realism" and deadpan absurdism. By introducing us to Arthur in an authentically bleak and rowdy jail, and then showing him getting bailed out by a wealthy client who needs help fixing

a potentially embarrassing situation, Jewison asks us to identify with Arthur's plight as a good man put upon by corruption, and to take his world and its inhabitants seriously as stand-ins for the world off screen. But what to make, then, of another early scene, in which a judge, who is coded as "good" by his friendship with Arthur, shoots a gun at the ceiling in his courtroom to break up a melee? Or a helicopter crash played for laughs? Or the also apparently intentionally comic scene in which Jay suffers a breakdown and throws an epic tantrum, using stacks of cafeteria plates as ammunition? Jewison takes pains to set up the realness of the film's world, and then peppers that world with impossible characters whose actions qualify as surreal.

With two of his three clients dead and the third revealed to be a rapist who will likely be protected by his own position of power while Arthur is disbarred, our hero is put through at least as much soul-crushing tragedy as Serpico, who was last seen at the end of *Serpico* alone, dejected, demoralized—having fully given up. The final scene of *Justice*, meanwhile, is even more cynical, suggesting that Arthur's only recourse will be to throw up his hands and laugh it all off. In other words, he can't beat them—and he certainly can't change them—so he might as well join them.

That Arthur starts near the mental and emotional point where Serpico left off, with his damaged psyche revealed to be a product of clearly heightened circumstances, made the character, and the performance, a punching bag for some critics, who were largely thrown by Jewison's strange blending of social commentary and exaggerated, often physical humor, his insistence on the real-world consequences of corruption delineated through the type of action that only happens in the movies. It was, as Pacino promised, something they had never seen before.

Paradoxically, while they were clearly unprepared for the strange hybrid nature of the film as a whole, a common complaint was that when it came to Pacino's performance, it was more of the same. "Much of it plays on a level of frenzied unreality, with only Pacino holding it together and giving it a little feeling," wrote David Denby. "Yet Pacino has been used badly. This old, old movie game of one-man-against-the-system is phony and sentimental and probably destructive... And isn't it a bit early for his ascension to Paul Muni's late-career status as the Pasteur-Zola-Last Angry Man of movies? It's a damn silly thing for an actor to want."[109]

Even those critics who acknowledged that Pacino was stepping out of his comfort zone had nothing friendly to say about it. "Pacino seems miscast—as a romantic lead, and also as an educated man under moral or intellectual stress," wrote Renata Adler in the *New Yorker*.[110] It's a comment that, today, almost smacks

of discrimination: Pacino, of course, was one of a handful of actors of his time who had broken ground in screen acting by giving leading men the face of the American everyman—identifiably the product of immigrant genes and urban upbringing, free of Hollywood cosmeticization or homogenization. And here was the *New Yorker* critic saying that putting such a face on a man who went to college and seduced a beautiful career woman was unbelievable.

The fundamental problem seemed to be the film's juxtaposition of "real" and "not real." "Our criminal justice system IS a shambles," acknowledged Andrew Sarris in the *Village Voice*, "but if we are knowledgeable enough to recognize this fact, we are long past the point when a big-star grandstand play can be taken seriously as a solution."[111] But Jewison doesn't seem to be suggesting that Pacino's grand-standing *is* a "serious solution." Nor, for that matter, does the film's comedy offer the escapist pleasures usually associated with cinematic laughs. ...*And Justice for All* is undeniably schizophrenic—but that schizophrenia is, in a way, the subject of the movie. The larger-than-life elements make perfect sense within the logic of the film, because the point is that the legal machine is so toxic that it eventually makes everyone trapped in it functionally insane. Within this logic, scenes that play as comic in the moment are seen in hindsight, at the end of the film, as tragic—products of an environment that has drifted so far off-kilter that traditional distinctions between right and wrong are meaningless, and sanity cannot be restored. In other words, in the world of the film, surreality *is* realism.

Audiences responded better than critics. *Justice* made $23 million in its first two months in release and was championed as one of the box-office hits of the season. That said, one of the film's more positive notices sounded an alarm that would prove to be fateful. "Pacino is very watchable and enjoyable," wrote critic Charles Champlin. "But it is also true that the actor does not totally disappear into the character, and his unabashed energy finally draws attention to the performer performing."[112] In that final courtroom blow-up, Pacino seems to be going through the motions of being Al Pacino: pacing back and forth, his little body slightly hunched over, as he did in *Dog Day Afternoon*, his vocal dynamics building from a calm indoor voice to an out-rageous bellow, a technique, as we've seen, he had used before and would use may times again. He didn't disappear into the role—the role disap-peared behind the screen persona of Al Pacino.

No longer the fresh-faced outsider, Pacino was moving into a new phase of his career, in which the characters he played often seemed to be vague entities in dialogue with, or even overpowered by, the known quantity of Al Pacino, which by now was familiar and consistent enough to read as a kind of shorthand. Pacino the actor was conscious of the dangers posed by Pacino the celebrity. "Actors are always outsiders," he said in 1979. "It's necessary to be able to interpret, and all that gets distorted when people become famous. Our roots were always outside; we're wayward vagabonds, minstrels, outcasts. And that may explain why so many of us want to be accepted into the mainstream of life. But when we are— here's the contradiction!—we sometimes lose our outsider's edge."[113]

6

Tony Montana

Scarface (1983)
Brian De Palma

"Man's reach should exceed his grasp, or what's a heaven for? That's a great expression, and I think that's Tony Montana." [114]
—Al Pacino, 2011

By the mid-1980s, Al Pacino was in something of a slump. His last film to please both audiences and critics had been *Dog Day Afternoon* in 1975. *...And Justice for All* had done well enough at the box office, but was savaged by the press, and it failed to ignite the zeitgeist the way earlier Pacino projects had. *Bobby Deerfield* (1977), *Cruising* (1980), and *Author! Author!* (1982) were all considered bombs. In between the last two films, Pacino had triumphed in a stage production of David Mamet's *American Buffalo*, first Off-Broadway and then on. But his film career was in need of a fix. *...And Justice for All*, wrote critic Gene Siskel was "the second bomb in a row (after *Bobby Deerfield*) for the previously remarkable Pacino. What has happened to his schlock-detector? After making the *Godfather* films and *Serpico*, why couldn't Pacino have smelled this one?" [115]

Looking at Pacino's life off screen in the second half of the 1970s offers a few clues as to how his "sense of smell" may have become so impaired. When Pacino had been making those movies that critics like Siskel approved of, the actor had been an increasingly nonfunctional alcoholic. Pacino would finally quit drinking for good in 1977. In 1979, he would credit old friend Charlie Laughton for making him realize his problem. Four years later, Pacino would admit, "I don't like to talk about the drinking, because it's something I don't quite understand. I wish I understood it more. We sometimes live a life and do things and are not aware that we're doing them." Pacino said that after Laughton forced him to recognize his problem, "it took me about a year to understand it and another year to get off it." [116]

Alcohol was not the only crutch that Pacino was forced to learn how to live without in the late 1970s and early 1980s. In 1982, Pacino lost a key mentor with the death of Lee Strasberg. Meanwhile, Pacino had fallen out with Marty Bregman, the manager who had discovered him and produced *Serpico* and *Dog Day Afternoon*. Bregman had secured European financing to produce Oliver Stone's *Born on the Fourth of July*, in which Pacino had agreed to star as Vietnam vet Ron Kovic. Pacino turned down offers to appear in *Coming Home* and *Days of Heaven*, grew a moustache, and started spending time with the real Kovic in preparation. Then, suddenly, the European financing disappeared, and Pacino backed out and signed on to *...And Justice for All* instead. According to Stone, the actor got cold feet. Pacino said he was only following the lead of William Friedkin, who had been attached to direct but had had to drop out over scheduling. But Bregman argued that Friedkin was never solidly attached and, having put money of his own into the movie already, he had been counting on Pacino's participation in order to secure further investment. With Pacino no longer attached, the movie was a no-go.

The incident caused a major rift between Pacino and Bregman; they stopped speaking. "Our relationship changed several years ago; then it finally just dissipated," Pacino said in 1979. "He became a producer. It wasn't the same anymore." [117] On his transition from manager to producer, Bregman didn't mince words: "I grew tired of playing nursemaid to gifted but insecure actors." [118]

In the end, it was Pacino who reached out to his former manager, to ask him to get involved in mounting a remake of *Scarface*. Doing press for the movie, Pacino indicated that their relationship was still difficult to define. "In some ways now, it's less complicated. I'm less the kid now, less the boy. But it always takes two. I don't want to get into 'He did this to me,' because it implies, 'I did that to him.' And I'm not completely over those feelings." [119]

A Brechtian Gangster Movie

It was no secret that Pacino had forever preferred to act on stage rather than on screen. "I'm more comfortable in a play. In film there's always a certain sense of control, of holding back. The stage is different; there's more to act." [120] His love of and experience in the theater, as well as his yen for "more to act," would together directly inform *Scarface*.

The actor had first heard of the original film, the 1931 gangster classic directed by Howard Hawks and starring Paul Muni, when he was

Al Pacino as Tony Montana
in Brian De Palma's *Scarface*
(1983).

95

appearing in and helping to mount a theatrical production of Bertolt Brecht's Hitler parable *The Resistible Rise of Arturo Ui* in 1975. "I knew that Bertolt Brecht was very interested in gangster movies," Pacino remembered later. In the process of developing Brecht's work, Pacino said, "We were looking at old thirties movies, and the one we were trying to get hold of was *Scarface*, and we couldn't get it."[121]

A few years later, Pacino was in Los Angeles for a shoot when he drove past a repertory theater on Sunset Boulevard and saw *Scarface* on the marquee. "I just went in and saw this great movie: it had a real feeling in it, a grand feeling. I thought it would be interesting to make a remake of this, in another way. So I called Marty Bregman, and he saw it and got very excited."[122]

Bregman, for his part, claimed credit for the inception of the idea—in the film's production notes, he said he saw the movie on late-night TV and envisioned Pacino in the part, and then hired first David Rabe and finally Oliver Stone to write the screenplay. And yet Bregman also admitted, "If Al gets excited about something, I get excited."[123]

No matter the origin, it was an ideal project to bring the old band back together. *Scarface* was a gangster picture, like *The Godfather*. And, like *Serpico* and *Dog Day Afternoon*, a topical drama inspired by real-life events (the Mariel mass immigration from Cuba to Florida, the emergence

of the violent South American drug cartels), with Pacino playing an antihero whose antisocial acts serve his personal moral code. And, Bregman hoped, like *Serpico* and *Dog Day*, it would be directed by Sidney Lumet. Lumet was instrumental in the early development of the movie—it was his idea to set the action in Miami, for instance—but he and Bregman ultimately disagreed on the film's direction, with Lumet taking particular issue with the script's "corny elements," including intimations that Tony Montana had incestuous feelings for his sister Gina.

"I don't know how Al felt at this stage, I never asked him," Lumet said. The filmmaker wanted to add in a political element, to introduce the idea of the "CIA's involvement in drugs as part of their anti-Communist drive. I didn't want to do it on just a gangster or cop level. As it stood, it was a comic strip."

"What he wanted to do was just preposterous," scoffed Bregman, who hired Brian De Palma to replace Lumet. "De Palma and I had no intention whatever of making a comic strip. We wanted to give the whole thing a larger-than-life *operatic* quality."[124] Pacino approved, saying of De Palma after the shoot, "The picture had a fire to it. That was part of Brian's concept, to do everything in an extraordinary way—to have the violence blown up, the language blown up. The spirit of it was Brechtian, operatic. It didn't opt for sentiment but had an almost fablelike quality to it."[125] In this case, "Brechtian" means that Tony Montana was not intended to be a character that the audience identified with, but instead looked at from an emotional remove. "He was always perceived as two-dimensional; that was the style," Pacino recalled. "It wasn't about *why* he does *what* he does."[126]

Larger Than Life

Tony Montana arrives in Miami in 1980, allowed a free pass from Cuba during the Mariel boatlift, when Jimmy Carter opened the Florida border to refugees—and Castro opened his prisons to send his country's baddest seeds overseas. Tony is literally marked as bad news by a scar on his cheek. Taken in for questioning by US officials, he insists, "[I'm] a political prisoner from Cuba, and I want my fuckin' human rights, now."

"Human rights" are not all Tony Montana wants; he'll later state the outsize ambition to own "the world and everything in it." But first, he has to get out of the refugee camp under a freeway overpass, where he's dumped alongside friends/fellow refugees Manny Ribera (Steven Bauer), Angel (Pepe Serna), and Chi-Chi (Ángel Salazar). Manny strikes a deal with a drug kingpin on the outside, Frank Lopez (Robert Loggia): Tony will commit a revenge murder on Frank's behalf inside the camp, and Frank will get the crew the green cards they need to get out.

Both sides make good on their promise. Once out, Tony and friends are assigned to complete a drug deal with a crew of Colombians. They show up at a motel room, where the Colombians murder Angel with a chainsaw in the bathtub. Tony is next; splattered with Angel's blood, facing down the buzzing weapon that killed his friend, he's so nonplussed that he looks half asleep. He blithely spits, "Fuck you!" It's an interesting twist on the Pacino crescendo and the power dynamics we've seen before. Here Tony has no real power, but is able to disarm his attacker, and thus save his own life by downplaying his emotions; thanks to Pacino's cool, calm delivery, Tony's foolish fearlessness reads as a clever mind game.

Tony and Manny survive, and take the drugs and the money directly to Frank. Having cheated death, Tony has an exaggerated swagger. "I need a guy who has steel in his balls, Tony," Frank says. "A guy like you." Indeed, Pacino walks as though his pelvis is made of metal and the camera is a magnet.

To cement their working relationship, Frank takes Tony to dinner at the Babylon Club, a massive disco with mirrored walls, which becomes center stage for the film's depiction of the intersection of debauchery, lawlessness, and greed. As they eat and drink, Frank indoctrinates Tony in his working philosophy. Saying the now-classic line, "Never underestimate the OTHER guy's greed," Loggia's voice, in volume and intensity, rises and falls like a bell curve. As the drug lord is teaching his new protégé, it's almost as if Pacino is learning, too: this vocal dynamic, which we'd seen versions of in *Serpico* and *Justice*, was increasingly becoming a key part of Pacino's repertoire of tools.

At that dinner, Tony meets Frank's trophy girlfriend, Elvira (Michelle Pfeiffer). Assigned to drive the lady, Tony demonstrates his bizarre charisma: behind the wheel, he takes a snort of coke and jumps on Elvira in the front seat. She pushes him away: "Listen, Tony, I don't fuck around with the help," Elvira sniffs. But, somehow, a moment later he has her giggling and smiling. As Tony courts his boss's girl, he runs into trouble with the other women in his life. He shows up suddenly at the tiny home of his mom and his younger, beautiful sister Gina (Mary Elizabeth Mastrantonio), flashing cash. While Gina is happy to take it, Mom cuts right to the chase: "Who did you kill for this, Antonio?" she demands to know. "It's Cubans like you who are giving a bad name to our people!"

The scene is key to the difference between Tony Montana and Pacino's previous, iconic gangster role, Michael Corleone. Michael is highly conscious of what message his actions broadcast to outsiders: his primary goal is to move the Corleone family out of the underworld and into the straight business world. But unlike Michael, Tony doesn't care about legitimacy, or legacy, or future generations. For Tony, unable to look beyond the moment, ruling the Miami underworld as a Cuban is victory enough.

There's a significant emotional difference, too, which is crucial to Pacino's extremely different approach to playing the two gangster kings. Michael's tragedy is that he is forced to cut off his humanity as a young man, only to spend a lifetime working his way "up" in mainstream society in an ultimately failed attempt to get that humanity back. Tony's tragedy is that he couldn't detach his emotions and personal desires, couldn't suppress himself in the interest of business. This manifests itself in a number of ways—from his gaudy, attention-grabbing cocaine-white suits and escalating drug use; to his insane overprotection of Gina, physically assaulting any man who dares touch her; to his refusal to follow through with a political assassination because it requires killing a woman and children.

Tony's feelings are as visible as the scar on his face, and the only power he has comes from his irrationality. Frank warns Tony early on to tone it down: "The guys who last in this business are the guys who fly straight, low-key, quiet," he says. "But the guys who want it all—chicas, champagne, flash—they don't last." Tony not only doesn't listen, he assassinates Frank, and usurps him. Michael's power comes from his inscrutability. In the *Godfather* films, men are

Top: Tony, Mama Montana (Miriam Colon), and Gina Montana (Mary Elizabeth Mastrantonio).

Bottom: Tony behind the wheel with Elvira Hancock (Michelle Pfeiffer).

Dinner at a swanky restaurant turns into a boozy, coke-fueled blowup.

Following pages: Al Pacino and Oliver Stone on the set of *Scarface*.

scared of Pacino's character because they don't know what he's thinking. In *Scarface*, they're afraid of Pacino's character because it's evident that he's not thinking, that he'll do whatever feels right in the moment, without assessing the consequences. He's scary because he's not afraid of the future.

The Method Behind the Monster

For all his many, many faults, Tony Montana is heroic by mere virtue of the fact that he has a personal code of ethics; he is true to himself and never hides that or pretends to be something he is not. These ethics underline many of the film's most memorable lines, which have survived to become catchphrases: "A man who ain't got his word is a cockroach," or, "You know what capitalism is? Getting fucked."

If these ethics are the core of the character, then the key scene of the film may be a monologue Pacino delivers late in the game. A dinner at a swanky restaurant has turned into a boozy, coke-fueled blowup, with Tony's now-wife Elvira storming away from the table. Having attracted the attention of the establishment's largely blue-haired clientele, he slurs, "You're all a bunch of fucking assholes. You know why? You don't have the guts to be what you wanna be." Tony stumbles to his feet and continues to address his audience, lurching from table to table: "You need people like me... Me, I always tell the truth. Even when I lie."

The scene, though as exaggerated as the chainsaw murder or the final, famous "Say 'ello to my lil' fren'" blowout, taps into a very real feeling. Bringing to life the repressed rage and angst of the capitalist who benefits from a broken system but is also trapped by it, Tony speaks sentiments shared by anyone who has been made to feel like an outsider by the prying eyes and judgment of strangers, anyone who has followed his own path and suffered the consequences. This monologue ties Pacino's whole unwieldy performance together, revealing that as cartoonish as it may be, there's genuine emotional truth running through all of it.

Many years later, a journalist would ask Pacino how he approached "Method-acting a monster" without losing track of art and life—without becoming a monster off camera. "One doesn't see it as a monster," Pacino replied. "You don't look at it like that. It's passion and emotions, and it's in all of us." Put that way, Tony Montana seems like the logical next step in Pacino's voice-of-male-frustration trajectory.

That said, he was conscious of not wanting to bring Tony home. "When I was doing *Scarface*, I remember being in love at that time," Pacino said in 2004. He didn't name the object of his affection, but it was likely actress Kathleen Quinlan, who was his live-in girlfriend in 1983.

"I was so glad it was at that time. I would come home and she would tell me about her life that day and all her problems and I remember saying to her, 'Look, you really got me through this picture,' because I would shed everything when I came home."[127]

"Hey, I've Never Done Cocaine and I'm Supposed to Know What It's Like..."

Pacino was quick to proclaim a personal connection to Tony Montana, in that they were both products of the immigrant experience. "Coming from the South Bronx, being, in a sense, Latin myself, I have a certain connection to the Latin feeling," he would say. "Although the Cuban thing is a difference."

A big difference: for the first time on screen, *Scarface* would require Pacino to adopt an accent to portray an ethnicity not his own. Given what Pacino had previously represented as an actor and as a movie star—a Method-guided reliance on lived experience, the emergence of the screen idol who looked and acted like a "real" person— the role would be more than an acting exercise. It would fundamentally change Pacino's screen image. "I was very inspired by Meryl Streep's work in *Sophie's Choice*," Pacino noted. "I thought that her way of involving herself in playing someone who is from another country and another world was particularly fine and committed and... courageous. It was very inspiring."[128]

After taking an extremely proactive role in the casting of the film (he fought to give the part of addict trophy wife Elvira, ultimately played by Michelle Pfeiffer, to the very different Glenn Close), Pacino moved down to Miami during preproduction to soak up the sound of the Cuban dialect. He spoke in his distinctive accent on and off set during production. The change in location helped to reconfigure Pacino's conception of the character. Originally, "all I wanted to do was imitate Paul Muni," Pacino confessed. "His acting went beyond the boundaries of naturalism into another kind of expression. It was almost abstract what he did. It was almost uplifting."[129] But knowing that he needed to do more than simply copy Muni, Pacino said he "was looking for a style. You see, what Muni had done was a base for me to start from; he gave such a solid foundation to the role, it was like a canvas. I knew it was a characterization I wanted to continue."[130]

Deeply involved with cocaine himself at the time, Oliver Stone had done extensive research in Miami, then quit drugs cold turkey and moved to Paris to write the screenplay. He designed the character as a combination of real people he had met in Miami, Muni's *Scarface*, and Humphrey Bogart's character in *The Treasure of the Sierra Madre* (in *Scarface*, that film is projected on a sheet in the refugee camp where Tony begins his life in America).

When he first saw Paul Muni in *Scarface,* Al Pacino said, "I knew it was a characterization I wanted to continue."[m] His performance in Brian De Palma's 1983 update of Howard Hawks's 1932 film indeed seems to start where the original, compromised by the need to appeal to the moralistic censors of the day, left off. Hawks's *Scarface* was released with a subtitle—"The Shame of the Nation"—and pre-titles informing the viewer that the film to follow was meant as a damnation of the scourge of organized crime. This is in sharp contrast to De Palma's operatic treatment, which exaggerated both the bloody toll of criminal capitalism and its rewards. The crucial similarity between the two portrayals is the likability the actors instill in men who are otherwise monstrous. Working under very different circumstances, both actors create characters the audience wants to identify as heroes, even as they commit heinous acts. In order for the film to function as anticrime propaganda, Muni's Italian immigrant Tony Camonte can't be evil incarnate—he's got to be a normal man who suffers for his bad decisions. Muni plays his scarred gangster as a lunkhead, both cocky and clownish in his menace and single-minded in his pursuit of desire. His Italian accent is exaggerated and inconsistent; his wide grin stretches across his face like pulled taffy. The overall effect is not to lionize Tony but almost to make the viewer feel sorry for him—he acts as though he's unaware of consequences because he simply doesn't know any better.

Pacino's performance isn't exactly subtle, and his Tony Montana is no more of a rational being, and yet his appeal is not in his frailty but in his bravado. The contrasts between the two performances are apparent in their different endings. Once his beloved sister is shot, Muni's Tony becomes manically terrified, and is ultimately contrite in the face of the final punishment, begging for mercy with shaky hands. Meanwhile, Pacino's Tony literally marches toward his death with guns blazing, taunting his attackers to go ahead and shoot, with Pacino giving no indication that the character has any doubt about his own invincibility. The Muni Tony's weakness is fear; the Pacino Tony rises and falls on his fearlessness. And where Muni's performance is all broadly sketched comedy and tragedy—his lack of shading fitting for a film that sees itself as a parable—Pacino the Method actor finds ways to ground the larger-than-life character in real, relatable emotion.

Opposite: Tony "Scarface" Camonte (Paul Muni) in *Scarface: The Shame of the Nation* (1932), directed by Howard Hawks.

Al Pacino said his own background made him feel closer to his Latino character.

Pacino's preparation was unusually collaborative. "I didn't do it alone; I had a lot of help," he noted. Tony Montana was built from the outside in. Pacino trained physically, to "get the kind of body I wanted for the part. I used the boxer Roberto Duran a little bit. There was a certain aspect of Duran, a certain lion in him, that I responded to in this character."[131]

After practicing the accent with his friend Charlie Laughton and dialect coach Bob Easton, he perfected it by conversing with Spanish-speaking members of the crew. "We would have long discussions out at my house about what the guy I was going to play would be like. It was the first time I opened the character up to a lot of people, which was helpful for me." A key consultant was Steven Bauer, the actor who played Tony's partner Manny in the film. "Being Cuban, he helped me with the language; he taped things for me, he told me things I wouldn't have known."[132] Bauer, who later described his first meeting with Pacino as "love at first sight," added, "He asked if I could teach him Spanish, and I said I could and also teach him the sense of humor of a people who've lost their country and who, like the Jews, laugh at our fate. He wanted to know about the mindset of being an exile."[133]

The accent was not the only area in which Pacino requested Bauer's help. "One of the first things Al came to me with was, 'Hey, I've never done cocaine and I'm supposed to know what it's like. Have you done it?'" Bauer remembered. He had, in fact, tried the drug. "I taught him all the nuances, the rituals, and whenever he did any scenes involving drugs, I'd be standing right by because he asked me, 'Watch me and make sure I look real.'"[134]

On set, in what was becoming a familiar story for Pacino, the star and his director clashed. "There wasn't the communication between Al and Brian that one would expect," Oliver Stone said in 2011. "Al liked being talked to, but Brian is from the Spielberg school, where it's all about the setup and getting the shot—and the shot takes fucking forever."[135] De Palma acknowledged the tension in the most diplomatic way possible— "It's very challenging to work with an actor who's as good as Pacino," he said[136]—and Bregman dismissed it. "If there were any shouting matches on *Scarface*, it was between Al and myself, and always over a creative matter."[137]

Over the Line

There's no question that the production itself was over the top, only partially by design, and that *Scarface* went over budget and behind schedule, due to De Palma and Pacino's warring perfectionism, as well as the delays that incurred when protests from Florida's Cuban community forced the shoot to move from Miami to Los Angeles.

But the filmmakers had more control over the movie's excessive content. The word "fuck" was used a then-record-breaking 226 times, once every 1.33 minutes.[138] The US ratings board initially gave the film an X, stirring up invaluable publicity. The rating was changed to R on appeal, after Universal paid two psychiatrists to testify at an appeal hearing that the film's violence would not cause permanent damage to teen viewers.

"It's somewhere between naturalism and opera," Pacino said before the film was released. At that point, he didn't seem fully aware that the performance would be read as camp in its excess. "You're always afraid that you may go over the line into caricature. I hope I haven't."[139]

"I'm not going back in any cage," Tony says, when prison seems like a real possibility. The same could be said for Pacino's performance style. With *Scarface*, Pacino went fully over the top— and he would stay there, the signature of his screen persona transforming from one based on restraint and internal realism to being exaggerated and external, not approximating life so much as parodying it.

Twenty years later, Pacino would talk about the importance of going big, as a method to get the performance right. "Certain roles you go too far," he said. "But part of what you hope to do is not censor yourself, and then find a way to pull back, and sometimes you don't censor yourself and you get caught off guard."[140]

Pacino trusted his director to tell him when he had gone too far, to help him modulate the performance. But sometimes directors don't want to pull an actor back from the edge— especially when that actor has an upper register as potentially transcendent as Al Pacino's. Certainly, in the case of *Scarface*, it seems that De Palma was trying to push both the performance and the production as far as it could go. Stone recollected that De Palma "added what seemed like 100 assassins" to Tony's death scene, which he had written as a comparatively spartan affair. "Brian was glamorizing that world to a large extent," the screenwriter said. "He isn't interested in reality. Things got bigger, which isn't necessarily a bad thing, but it's a Hollywood thing."[141]

The bigness, the drift away from reality, in Pacino's performance as Tony Montana seemed to set a new bar for what he could do—and what he was expected to do—on screen. In 1975, Pacino had been accused by a theater critic of plagiarizing himself—his performance in *Arturo Ui*, the Brecht play that led to his interest in *Scarface*, wrote Arthur Friedman, was "a faded carbon copy" of Pacino's rendition of the title part in a previous production of *Richard III*.[142] But as time went on, increasingly it seemed like Pacino was expected to repeat himself. In 2004, Pacino was asked if he's ever had a director say, "Give me more Pacino." The actor responded with a roar. "Yeaaaaaah. That has happened, yes."[143]

Whatever one might think of the film, it's hard to argue against the fact that in *Scarface* Pacino produced a performance that was unlike anything the audience had seen from him before. But as the actor aged, often it seemed like "going big" was his default—a way of bringing to life both intentionally cartoonish characters like Big Boy in *Dick Tracy* (1990) and Satan in *Devil's Advocate* (1997), and ostensibly "real" people such as Colonel Slade in *Scent of a Woman*. His ability to go over the top, to "act more," would almost become synonymous with his name.

Ahead of Its Time

"Nothing develops in Pacino's performance," complained usual De Palma supporter Pauline Kael, in a pan that was typical of the reviews written about *Scarface*. "Most of the time here he goes through the motions of impersonating a dynamo while looking as drained as he did at the end of *The Godfather Part II*... He's doing the kind of Method acting in which the performer wants you to see that he's living the part and expects you to be knocked out by his courage in running the gauntlet. Pacino is certainly willing to go all the way with Tony's drunken and drugged-out loutishness. But... he's hollow from the start—he seems to have to act to look alive."[144]

Many critics didn't buy Pacino's transformation. "He gives a studied, mannered performance that commands the spectator watch and judge," wrote Enrique Fernandez in the *Village Voice*. "I didn't see Tony Montana. I saw Al Pacino." Fernandez's colleague Andrew Sarris also criticized Pacino by crediting the actor as the author of the performance: "One wonders if Oliver Stone actually 'wrote' the script, or if Pacino made it up as he went along."[145] Richard Corliss was one of few who appreciated the growth that the performance represented. "[Pacino] creates memories of earlier performances," Corliss acknowledged in *TIME*, "...but creates his freshest character in years."[146]

Scarface grossed about $40 million on initial release, which would be about $86 million today. It wasn't a bomb, but it wasn't one of the top ten grossers of the year (a year that included *Return of the Jedi* and *Flashdance*), and, nominated for zero Oscars, it certainly wasn't respected.

"*Scarface* wasn't understood," Pacino would say later. "It was about excess and avarice and everything being out of proportion. The character didn't try to explain himself."[147] The film became understood in time, particularly within hip-hop culture, to the extent that when *Scarface* was rereleased on DVD in 2003, the film was packaged with a new documentary called *Origins of a Hip-Hop Classic*, featuring interviews with rap-world legends such as Russell Simmons, Sean Combs, and Snoop Dogg.

Top: Tony Montana seemed to set a new bar for what Al Pacino could do as an actor.

Bottom: Tony Montana and Manny Ribera.

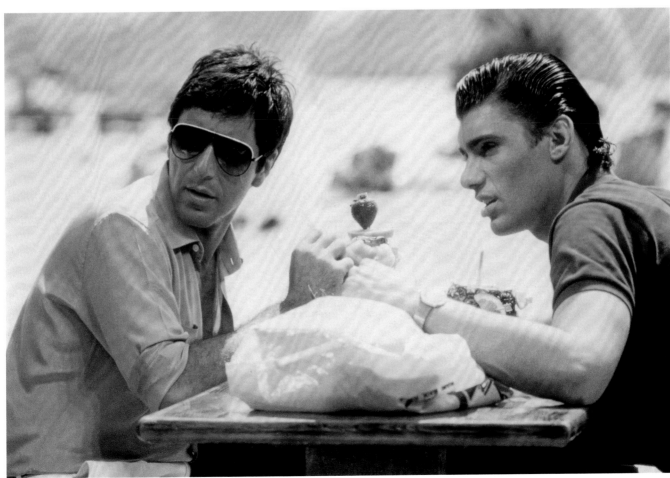

Tony and his sister Gina.

Opposite: "Say 'ello to my lil' fren'".

It's also the rare film to spawn a phenomenon that gets bigger over time. The film's story was continued in the hit 2006 video game *Scarface: The World Is Yours* (for which Pacino declined to provide his own voice, and was replaced by video-game actor André Sogliuzzo). In 2008, the Los Angeles Film Festival hosted a "swear-along screening" of the film in a 1,200 seat amphitheater.

"You make a lot of pictures, and you realize some don't have it," Pacino said in 2003. "I knew there was a pulse to this picture; I knew it was beating. And then I kept getting residuals from the movie, kept getting checks. And wherever I was filming, in Europe, people would come up to me and say, 'Hey, Tony Montana.' In Israel the Israelis came up to me and wanted to talk about *Scarface*. The Palestinians wanted to talk about *Scarface*."[148]

After the Opera

Following *Scarface*, Pacino was worn out, exhausted by the performance itself, and the media's outrage against the film. "I got pounded," Pacino said in 2011. "It was a pretty tough time for me." It didn't help that his next film, 1985's *Revolution*, was considered an unredeemable disaster comparable to Michael Cimino's *Heaven's Gate*. "It affected me to the point that, after *Scarface* and *Revolution*, I didn't make a movie again for four years."[149]

It hadn't exactly been the ecstatic reunion Pacino and Bregman were hoping for, and their relationship remained complicated. "[Bregman] loves Al," said Stone, "but he referred to him as a madman, a nutcase."[150] But when that madman decided to return to the screen after a four-year hiatus, it was in a Bregman production.

7

Frank Keller

Sea of Love (1989)
Harold Becker

"It is the very nature of fame that the light is on you a lot. I sort of wanted to turn the light out of my face... so I could see."[151]
—Al Pacino, 1991

In the 1970s, Al Pacino starred in eight films, five of which earned him Oscar nominations. Along with Robert De Niro, Dustin Hoffman, and Gene Hackman, he was part of a wave of theater-trained actors whose evident ethnicity and/or less-than-traditional movie-star personas helped to redefine the notion of celebrity and usher a more naturalistic performance style into Hollywood movies. It was, by any standard, a momentous decade.

In the 1980s, Pacino starred in only five films, none of which earned him an Oscar nomination. Four of those movies—*Cruising* (1980), *Author! Author!* (1982), *Scarface* (1983), and *Revolution* (1985)—were perceived at the time of release as flops, and only *Scarface* has been fully reclaimed in the decades since. The fifth film, 1989's *Sea of Love*, marked a rebirth for Pacino in more ways than one.

Pacino's absence from screens in the 1980s may have owed in part to squabbles with directors, including one on the set of *Author! Author!* with director Arthur Hiller, which was widely reported in the press—a rarity in those days. As Paul Rosenfield wrote shortly after the release of *Revolution*, "Much of Pacino's reputation, at least in the 1980s, rests on this experience. It's unusual for a major star to tiff so publicly with a director; a troublesome actor is not attractive in the cost-conscious '80s."[152]

Pacino would later describe the hiatus from Hollywood as "probably the most helpful thing I've ever done. I didn't even know I was doing it, it wasn't a conscious decision. I sort of felt that I wanted to go back to stuff I was familiar with, and develop a little in some way. Then four years had gone by and I was broke!"[153]

Pacino has made variations on this comment several times, apparently not at all shy to admit that he made *Sea of Love* primarily for the paycheck. Whatever his intention, the film was a much-needed critical and commercial hit. That success rehabilitated Pacino's standing in Hollywood; the movie ended up allowing Pacino to reinvent himself.

"Very Angsty"

"*Sea of Love* was about a guy going through crisis," Pacino said, "which I thought was interesting—to play a cop who's so caught up in his own survival he doesn't realize that his needs are so great they take precedence over his logic."[154] Those needs—personal, emotional, sexual—are the true subject of the movie. *Sea of Love* is packaged as an erotic thriller about a detective who is seduced by a possible killer of men, but the screenwriter, Richard Price, said that wasn't exactly the movie he set out to write. "There's not one word in it that I didn't write, but when I saw it, I was all freaked out," he said. "I never mean it to be a 'thriller.' I mean it to be two hours of high mopery. Very angsty."[155]

Pacino has said that he and costar Ellen Barkin "spent a couple of days just transcribing improvisations,"[156] which might call into question Price's claim that the film doesn't include a word he didn't write. But, in fact, the film is ultimately much more successful when considered a character study of a man in a midlife crisis who, having lost his grip on his own existence, has to redefine his priorities and his personality. In other words, it was a mirror of what Pacino himself was going through.

Sea of Love is a late-twentieth-century noir melodrama that, in the tradition of midcentury noir melodramas such as *Mildred Pierce* (1945) and *In a Lonely Place* (1950), is emblematic of its time and place—in this case, late-1980s Manhattan. But, like Michael Curtiz's and Nicholas Ray's florid dramas of the human heart, *Sea of Love* is also in a way a work of emotional surrealism about extremities of feeling that is distinctly outside real-world notions of era and geography.

The New York in which *Sea of Love* was set and partially shot—the city Al Pacino lived in and loved, and was loath to leave for long— was in the midst of one of its greatest recessions. After the Black Monday stock market crash of October 1987, Wall Street hemorrhaged jobs, which led to major losses in both commercial and residential real estate, destroying the local construction industry. As New York's fortunes were falling, its crime rate was steadily rising. The 2,246 murders reported in New York

Al Pacino as Frank Keller in Harold Becker's *Sea of Love* (1989).

in 1989, the year *Sea of Love* was released, was the highest since 1980—which, coincidentally, was the last time Al Pacino starred as a cop investigating sexually motivated murders, in *Cruising*. Today that film acts as a time capsule, documenting New York just before the city was transformed by new money, while marking the last of Pacino's performances as an idealistic young man whose vision of the world would, over the course of a film, be irreparably changed by an encounter with power.

Just as the New York of the late-1980s had devolved from a metropolis on the brink of a boom to a place plagued by unemployment, littered with vacant real estate, and haunted by violent crime, compared to the Al Pacino of 1980, the Al Pacino of 1989 was preternaturally decayed. The actor and the city were perfectly matched to the story. *Sea of Love* would bring into focus a long-term shift in the prototypical Pacino role. Once typecast as brooding young men whose dreams are dashed by authority, he had evolved into a wizened veteran who begins the film detached and disillusioned, and, over the course of the narrative, finds a source of hope to embrace, and essentially comes back to life.

This was as much a side effect of Pacino's advancing age as it was a sign of the times, reflecting a major evolution from the Hollywood of the mid-1970s to the Hollywood of the late 1980s and early 1990s, from auteur-driven,

European-influenced films about real lives to money-driven films set in impossible worlds with improbable outcomes. It was almost as if the success of *Star Wars* and other fantasy blockbusters had the pernicious effect of changing narrative expectations: no matter what, heroes could only prevail.

"Like a Fucking Teenager"

Pacino plays Detective Frank Keller, a twenty-year NYPD veteran deep in the throes of a midlife crisis. Problematically attached to the bottle, one night he drunk-dials his ex-wife; another night, at a policeman's banquet, he persuades a colleague he barely knows (played by John Goodman) to perform a striptease, and goads his partner (Richard Jenkins) into punching him. That the partner happens to be married to Keller's ex-wife brings the self-destruction full circle.

Pacino's Keller and Goodman's Queens-based Detective Sherman Touhey, eventually team up to try to crack a case. A number of men have been found dead, naked in bed, shot in the head from behind. The investigation suggests that all of the victims have placed personal ads in the same newspaper, all of them poetic in nature. Presuming that the perp is a woman who found and dated each of the men via the classifieds, Keller suggests that the cops place a similar ad in the paper, set up dates with all the ladies who answer, get their

fingerprints and match them to a cigarette butt found at the scene of one of the killings, and voilà—case closed.

The sting is set up in a bustling Midtown Manhattan restaurant. Pacino plays the supposed lonely heart, while Goodman dons an apron to deliver—and more importantly, retrieve—glasses of wine to a succession of women lured via personal ad. Keller tells his "dates" that he owns a printing press, a lie that one of them sees right through. "You have cop's eyes," she sniffs, getting up to leave. "If you're a printer, I've got a dick." Keller's barely under-his-breath comeback is indicative of his attitude toward women—"I didn't doubt it for a minute, baby."

Helen (Ellen Barkin), a big-haired blonde in a red leather jacket, doesn't finger Frank as a cop, but she does suspect they're not a match. Helen believes in "animal attraction," she tells her beleaguered date. She doesn't feel it with him, she says, and walks out without touching her glass of wine. Helen's positioning of herself as a wild animal and her apparent caution regarding leaving prints make her a viable suspect.

She also clearly sparks Frank's interest. A few days later, he runs into her on the street. They close down a bar and drunkenly stumble back to his place. In the middle of a steamy make-out session, she repairs to the restroom and Frank catches a glimpse of a gun in her purse. When she returns, he pushes her against the wall and

questions her about the piece—which turns out to be fake, a decoy the single woman carries to scare off would-be predators. Frank's suspicions are quelled, and Helen spends the night. The next morning, she leaves fingerprints on a glass before making her exit. Frank starts to put the glass in a bag to take to the station—and then pauses. He knows the evidence would be considered tainted, based on how it was acquired. He wipes the glass clean.

Frank and Helen begin seeing each other regularly, even as the lonely heart investigation continues. Sherman, well aware that his coinvestigator is sleeping with a woman they once suspected of being the enemy, urges Frank to get her prints, just so they can rule out her involvement. But as much as this would be the rational thing to do, Frank isn't thinking rationally. "I feel like a fucking teenager," he admits. Indeed, Keller throws himself into the affair with the crazed fervor of a man inexperienced in love. He's even able to momentarily forget how he and his new love met—but only momentarily. Clouded by paranoia, his sense dulled by drink, he acts erratically. One minute, within what seems like days of dating, he's asking Helen, a single mom, to move in with him. The next, he's lashing out at her, pressing her to talk about past lovers—particularly those she met via the personals.

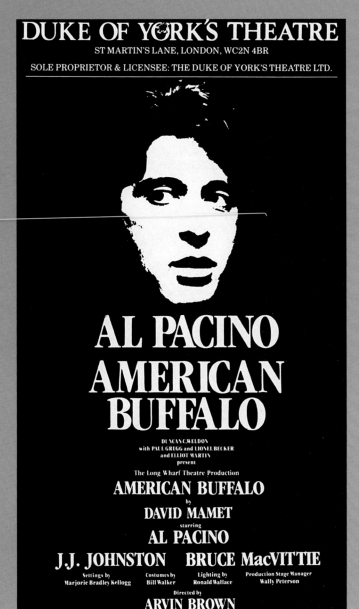

When Al Pacino was in his twenties, he started appearing on stage, and the experience of performing for a live audience changed him. "I could speak for the first time," he remembered later. "The characters would say these things that I could never say, things I've always wanted to say, and that was very liberating for me."[n] Movie stardom was an afterthought; by the time Pacino became a household name with *The Godfather*, he had already won a Tony for his lead role in the 1969 production of *Does a Tiger Wear a Necktie?* During the early years of his screen stardom, theater became a refuge for Pacino, a place to hone his craft and get his head together between films. "I went back to the stage because it was my way of dealing with the success I had, my way of coping," Pacino said in 1979. "It was a way of escaping the responsibility of what was happening."[o] He won another Tony in 1977 for his performance in David Rabe's *The Basic Training of Pavlo Hummel*, but his turn as the title character in a 1979 production of *Richard III* was not warmly received. Pacino was not doing it for the reviews. "Sometimes I spend full days doing Shakespeare by myself, just for the joy of reading it, saying those words," he disclosed at the time. "It's great therapy."[p] Those potentially therapeutic qualities must have been attractive to Pacino in the 1980s, when he turned to theater during a low point in his film career. He headlined a 1983 Broadway revival of David Mamet's *American Buffalo* and later, on a four-year hiatus from making Hollywood films, he concentrated on theatrical acting. He workshopped small plays, and starred in a production of *Julius Caesar* mounted as part of the New York Shakespeare Festival. Then there was *The Local Stigmatic*, a play in which Pacino had originally appeared Off-Broadway in 1969. Immediately after returning from the *Revolution* shoot in 1985, Pacino began workshopping a production of *Stigmatic* with director David Wheeler and the Theatre Company of Boston, starring himself and Paul Guilfoyle. This was filmed and eventually released on DVD (in 1990). *Stigmatic*, Pacino would say, "got me in touch with things I remembered as a young actor working: trying to really pick through things and find an expression of some sort." But then, "I turned around and I was broke. That was a rude awakening, and I had to go back to work."[q] After returning to the screen in *Sea of Love* and winning the Oscar for *Scent of a Woman*, Pacino began working on a personal project that would use film to explore a great work of theater; his film directorial debut, the self-described "docudrama" *Looking for Richard* (1996), is a highly personal exploration of Pacino's acting process. Pacino took up his beloved Shakespeare again through a much-ballyhooed return to Broadway in 2010 as Shylock in *The Merchant of Venice*. Meanwhile, Pacino has spent much of the past decade embroiled in an ever-evolving production of Oscar Wilde's *Salomé*, beginning with a staged reading on Broadway in 2003 and then reborn as a Los Angeles stage production costarring Jessica Chastain in 2006, which Pacino documented for a *Looking for Richard*–style film called *Wilde Salomé* that premiered at the 2011 Venice Film Festival.

Opposite: Al Pacino and director Harold Becker on the set of *Sea of Love*.

Harold Becker eyes a shot.

In attempting to be emotionally honest, he forgets to lie to her, revealing that the night they met he was on the job and she walked into a sting. Shaky, red-faced, and slit-eyed—drunk on booze and what Helen would call "animal attraction"—he makes a confession of love. "I can't even sleep in my bed, unless you're in it." It's too much, and she's scared of him. She doesn't understand that he's still unsure whether or not he should be scared of her.

They separate on bad terms. Frank goes home, and his place is broken into by Helen's ex-husband—he's been following the men Helen dates back to their apartments, forcing them to strip and murdering them. Frank and the ex struggle, and the perp crashes through the bedroom window, falling to his death.

Fade in to a coda. Frank and Sherman meet in a bar, apparently their first meeting in weeks. Frank orders a club soda—he's quit drinking in the interim. Sherman asks about Helen. Frank is visibly shaken talking about their now-nonexistent relationship. "What does anybody see in anybody?" Frank asks rhetorically. "People are work. Too much work."

Cut to the shoe store where Helen works. Frank waits outside for her. When she sees him, she tries to walk past without making eye contact. He follows her. He tells her he's quit drinking. He asks for a second chance. "The person you got involved with, that was half of me," he says. "You owe it to yourself to get to know the complete person." She asks if he still drinks coffee. "Like it's going out of style," he responds, with a big smile on his face. They continue walking together, eventually disappearing into a New York crowd.

"Mr. Pacino" Finds Himself in Frank

In 1988, Al Pacino spent some time with director Harold Becker working on a script called *Johnny Handsome*, about a criminal who gets extensive plastic surgery. They weren't able to fix it to Pacino's satisfaction, and both parties moved on (the film was eventually made by Walter Hill, starring Mickey Rourke). Around the same time, Pacino read a script called *Sea of Love*, which he forwarded on to Marty Bregman, who felt the script needed too much work. That project fell under the auspices of Universal, and the studio later asked Bregman to produce. He agreed to work with Richard Price on rewrites, to turn an angsty tale of a sad-sack, past-his-prime detective into a real mystery.

If nothing else, recovering alcoholic Pacino related to Keller's largely self-inflicted drunken misery. "The booze makes you susceptible to that insanity that happens to people when they fall in love," he said, effectively summing up the character's source of loneliness and vulnerability.[157]

After Pacino and Bregman's first choice of director, Sydney Pollack, passed, they went to Harold Becker, who, despite a spotty track record, Pacino remembered fondly from their work-shopping of *Johnny Handsome*. Interiors were filmed, at Universal's fiscally minded insistence, in Toronto, but eventually the production moved to Manhattan to shoot exteriors on the streets whose own angst would provide a meaningful subtext to the drama of the film. One anecdote from the shoot demonstrates that Pacino the actor was able to easily override his director as the driving creative force behind the film. "You don't talk to Mr. Pacino when he's working," a doorman at a Manhattan building where some of the film was shot told the *New York Times*. He also recalled watching one take, after which Becker told Pacino he had what he needed. "That vein in Mr. Pacino's forehead began pulsing, and he looked right at the director and said, 'One more time,' and the director said, 'Fine, Al,' and they did it one more time."[158]

The Weight of Age

The scene in which Frank and Helen meet occurs more or less at the midpoint of the movie, and it essentially bifurcates *Sea of Love* into two extremely distinct chunks. The first is the story of a veteran police detective struggling to accept and adapt to sudden bachelorhood, and professional seniority, in middle age. A functioning alcoholic and workaholic, he finds an enabler of both addictions in Goodman's slightly younger character, and the film seems dedicated to a relatively naturalistic examination of how these two men respond to each other, and their shared cynicism as seen-it-all defenders of a city in crisis.

When Keller meets Helen, *Sea of Love* breaks free of even a tangential relationship to reality. What was once a matter-of-fact procedural and behavioral study becomes a lurid erotic thriller and hyperreal exploration of a psyche. The film moves from objectively depicting a recognizable external world to assuming a highly subjective, internalized point of view, as Keller's own perspective transitions from hardened realism to romantic madness. Fittingly, Pacino's performance changes, too: he moves from low-key naturalism to extreme, hyperstylized emoting.

To match the strange, swoony fatalism of the Pacino character, there is a fin de siècle feel to the New York of the movie. The running motif of 45 records—Helen collects them; the killer leaves a single of the title track on the turntable at one of the crime scenes—serves as a marker of a swiftly disintegrating past that the characters have nostalgia for even before it has fully elapsed.

And Pacino seems to carry with him, on screen, the weight of the memory of the past. As in many Pacino films (the earlier *Cruising*, the later *Heat*),

those who enforce the law and those who break it are posited as being, in a sense, denizens of the same subculture. In the opening scene, Pacino and his partners, ever fans of the theatrical trap, lure dozens of criminals with outstanding warrants into a sting by inviting them to a neon-lit auditorium for a "breakfast with the Yankees." The cops pour the crooks screwdrivers as they are arresting them, so that they can join the officers in a toast to Keller's years on the job. (Keller's alcoholism is not out of place within what is depicted as a conspicuously hard-partying police force.) And Keller demonstrates an understanding of the less than black-and-white nature of right and wrong from the very beginning. When a latecomer arrives at the tail end of the roundup with his little kid in tow, Pacino's character discreetly turns him away so that he won't get sent to jail in front of his son. This act shows shades of both Serpico's and Arthur Kirkland's habit of putting human decency above protocol, as well as Tony's refusal in *Scarface* to kill a man if it means also harming his children.

When attempting to reunite with Helen, Frank stresses that his abstinence from alcohol has changed their circumstances, admitting that he had only previously allowed her to know one half of his bifurcated self. We've seen Pacino play a split personality before—Michael Corleone the war hero/lover/husband versus Michael Corleone the gangster/killer; Lion before and after the psychotic break in *Scarecrow*; the double lives of the undercover cops in *Cruising* and *Serpico*; the fatally ambiguous and ambivalent Sonny in *Dog Day Afternoon*. But in giving the actor an opportunity to address this duality directly, via dialogue in the film's denouement, *Sea of Love* turned what had been the subtext underlining Pacino's screen persona into its top-level subject. Just like the character he played, Pacino was, in essence, confronting the man he had been in order to move on.

"Pacino himself is not so young anymore, and the extra weight he's carrying doesn't flatter a man his height," observed David Denby in *New York* magazine. "Like Frank Keller, he badly needs to make a comeback (fourteen years have passed since *Dog Day Afternoon*), and it's fun to watch him use his worn, sagging body as the greatest gift an actor could be given, scoring point after point with a hoarse voice, a shambling walk, a tired, battered face electrified by bright, dark eyes—hot circuits to the brain passing through a surrounding deadness. Growling Price's bitter, bottom-of-the-shot-glass lines, Pacino is the soul of the picture."[159]

Denby was not the only critic to declare Pacino's return a success. "The zonked, mealy-mouthed performances he gave in films like *Bobby Deerfield* and *Cruising* seemed embalmed," wrote Peter Rainer. "In *Sea of Love*, he's got some of his fire back; a joy of acting comes through."[160]

Price, wrote David Ansen, had "given Pacino a role that reminds us why he was, back in the era of *Serpico* and *Dog Day Afternoon*, one of the treasures of American movies."[161]

Sea of Love grossed $10 million in its first weekend and was considered a huge hit. In collaboration with Marty Bregman, Pacino had finally emerged on the other side of a long professional crisis, riding out the period between youth and advanced age to emerge triumphant, once again on the A-list of actors who combined serious craft with commercial appeal.

What was he doing here that he hadn't done just a few years earlier, in *Cruising*, *Scarface*, or *Revolution*? It's possible that audiences and critics responded to an evident self-awareness — exacerbated by the passage of time between films and the signs of age marked on the actor's face — which Pacino seemed to be bringing to the screen for the first time. For years, Pacino had been accused by some critics of lazily playing "Al Pacino" — and those accusations would only increase over time — but in *Sea of Love*, Pacino seemed to be bringing himself into the performance quite intentionally. He saw himself in the role.

"I'm kind of lucky to go out there and play a character who mirrors what I'm feeling at the time," Pacino admitted. "I guess playing the part now, as opposed to playing it ten years ago, I have a closer understanding, a more tactile understanding of the character... He gets the sense that time is running out. He has a one-way ticket, the train is coming out of the tunnel and he sees, in the distance, the big mountain of mortality. And he wants to make his time here count."[162]

As Pacino biographer Andrew Yule writes, "Even in the movie's darkest scenes an element of self-mockery had been added that was absent before"[162] in Pacino's screen performances. In allowing himself to be seen through (or, depending on your point of view, superimposed over) the character, Pacino was in a sense building on the Brechtian aspect of *Scarface*. Yule cites Pacino's self-mockery as a point of praise. But, as Pacino watchers would become aware, it's a slippery slope between self-mockery and self-parody.

8

Lt. Colonel Frank Slade

Scent of a Woman (1992)
Martin Brest

"I'm gonna kill you, boy. Because I can't bear the thought of you SELLING OUT!!!"
—Frank Slade

As of this writing, Al Pacino has been nominated for eight Oscars and has won just one, for his performance as Frank Slade, the blind, suicidal former army colonel who goes on a weekend tour of Manhattan under the care of a naïve teenager in Martin Brest's 1992 drama, *Scent of a Woman*. To some, the fact that Pacino, one of the definitive representatives of 1970s American New Wave and all that it stood for in terms of changing the face of Hollywood, should have had to wait twenty years after the release of *The Godfather* for such recognition—and then, to get it for a film widely considered to be mediocre, even when he was also nominated the very same year for the much more highly esteemed *Glengarry Glen Ross*—is a travesty. Even Pacino himself seems determined to downplay the circumstances of this achievement: the biography of Pacino distributed to press covering his 1996 directorial debut, *Looking for Richard*, dismissed Brest's film as an "uneven, unabashed star showcase." As critic Tom Carson wrote in 2004, "Copping an Oscar for *Scent of a Woman* isn't the type of acclaim likely to give an actor much respect for the business he's chosen."[164]

Carson's choice of words is apt — in this context, acting is not Pacino's "art form" or "calling" or even "profession" but his "business," the rendering of services in exchange for money. And for that matter, it's not hard to see the Academy's decision to honor Pacino for *Scent of a Woman* as having more to do with bottom lines and best corporate practices than with artistry. It's not just that, with a $63 million North American gross (and over $100 million internationally), *Scent of a Woman* was a huge hit, the third-highest-grossing film of Pacino's career to that point after *The Godfather* and *Dick Tracy*. The film is also, in its test-marketed substance—or lack thereof—a validation of the triumph of businessmen in Hollywood, of filmmaking by committee of bean counters, over the auteurist challenge to the studio system represented by Pacino and his compatriots in the 1970s. By the early 1990s, Pacino had spent much of the previous decade on sabbatical from Hollywood, seeking refuge in the theater after a string of films that failed to catch on with audiences—box-office success being, in post-blockbuster Hollywood, the only metric of quality that mattered. His very willingness to make a milquetoast holiday-season release such as *Scent* was a sign that the actor was now more than willing to work on the industry's terms.

Sniffing Out Vulnerability

Scent of a Woman is established at the outset as the story of Charlie Simms (Chris O'Donnell), a high school senior at an exclusive Massachusetts boarding school. Thanksgiving weekend is approaching, and while his classmates, including political scion George Willis Jr. (Philip Seymour Hoffman), are looking forward to a pricey getaway at a ski resort in Vermont, Charlie is seen scouring the school's job board. A working-class kid attending the school on scholarship, Charlie is hoping to earn some money for a plane ticket in order to travel home to Oregon for Christmas.

Skiing is not the only distraction Charlie's spoiled peers have been planning. Charlie and George exit the library one night before Thanksgiving break to find a few of George's pals up on a ladder, affixing a balloon to a light post. The next morning, with the entire student body gathered around, the balloon explodes, dousing the headmaster's brand new sports car with white paint. The headmaster knows Charlie and George are innocent—but he also knows they were in a position to see who was responsible. He tells the boys that, come Monday morning, if they haven't ratted out the guilty parties, he'll expel them both. As an added incentive to go turncoat, Charlie is told that if he reveals the vandals, the headmaster will grease his path into Harvard, his college of choice.

One of the posts on the job board, advertising for a temporary minder for a "homebound relative," leads Charlie to the home of the Rossis, a middle-class family of four. Karen Rossi explains that her Uncle Frank has recently been discharged from a veteran's hospital and, with nowhere else to go, has been living in the Rossis' guesthouse. She leads Charlie through her backyard, and before they even enter the little house where Frank lives, they can hear him yelling vulgarities at a cat. Before leaving the wide-eyed teenager alone

Al Pacino as Lieutenant Colonel Frank Slade in Martin Brest's *Scent of a Woman* (1992).

with her uncle for a job interview, she promises, "Down deep, the man is a lump of sugar."

Charlie's first meeting with Frank is shot largely from the boy's perspective. At first it seems that the older man sitting across the room in an armchair, shouting invectives (he calls Charlie both an idiot and a moron before the boy has had a chance to speak a full sentence), has fixed the teenager with a fierce stare. But then the camera moves in for a medium shot of Pacino, and the actor—without breaking his monologue, his face still fixed in O'Donnell's direction—begins groping around first to find the bottle of Jack Daniel's on the table to his left, and then to meet the spout with a glass. The effect, one that Brest will replicate a number of times throughout the film in various ways, is to demonstrate that for all of his verbal rage, Slade's blindness makes him impotent, that his aggression and bravado are twinned with loneliness and vulnerability. Pacino is lit as if by a shaft of light coming through the window, so that when he yells, the spit spraying out of his mouth is illuminated in key light. He's a monster. He's also helpless. In classic Pacino protagonist fashion, the two sides of his dual personality work against each other, his extroverted nature underlining his lack of power, and that very conflict is what makes Slade human.

Other aspects of his personality are, shall we say, less realistic. *Scent of a Woman*'s key sentiments—that compassion heals all wounds; that every son needs a father, and vice versa—are undeniably traditional. But, as if in an attempt to mask its essential conservatism with "raw" theatricality, the film paves the road to its traditional mores with vulgarity. To Charlie's surprise, once the Rossis leave town for the weekend, Slade informs him that they're taking a trip to Manhattan. On the way out the door, Frank offers his cat a bit of parting advice: "Remember, when in doubt, fuck." On the plane, Frank gives a long, self-congratulatory monologue justifying the film's title,[165] about his love of the female anatomy. "Tits, hoo-ah!" Pacino bellows. "Mmm, legs. I don't care if they're Greek columns, or secondhand Steinways. What's between 'em... passport to heaven. Yes, Mr. Simms, there's only two syllables in the whole wide world worth hearing: pus-sy. Hah! Are you listening to me, son? I'm giving you pearls here!"

Every time a woman is in Slade's vicinity, Pacino twitches, as if Frank's nondisabled senses are stirring. The image alone is simply creepy; no wonder Brest lays on the treacly score, to sentimentalize the threat. The film seems to want to send the message that this dirty old man's hunger for women is a weakness, and thus a vulnerability, and thus a reason for our sympathy. It worked, at least on mainstream audiences. During the time of its release, the most talked about scene in the film was the tango Pacino performs with the much-younger actress Gabrielle Anwar, which

Top: Slade takes Charlie on a trip into Manhattan.

Bottom: Playing a blind man takes one of Al Pacino's greatest acting tools—his eyes—away from him.

was read as legitimately seductive: Pacino literally danced his way into viewers' hearts.

Learning to dance the tango was just part of Pacino's highly physical approach to the role. Playing a blind man who spends the bulk of his screen time either wearing dark glasses or gazing blankly meant that Pacino lost access to his eyes, which from *The Godfather* to *Sea of Love* had been his most reliable tool for adding depth and irony to even thinly written material. Just as a blind man learns to more strenuously exploit his remaining senses, Pacino amplifies the assets he has left: his body and his voice. Pacino's Frank walks hunched at the neck, his shoulders and face often so stiff you could mistake the character's disability for palsy or paralysis. In contrast, his voice is all over the place—his twinge of Southern accent inconsistent, statements crescendoing up as if at random. These elements combine to form a bizarrely mesmerizing presence. Pacino's Frank doesn't exactly communicate; instead, he storms into spaces and changes the temperature in the room. But because the performance maintains such an even level of overkill, Pacino is only really affecting in rare moments of reflection.

The second half of the film offers a number of major set pieces for Pacino's showboating. Frank has not concealed from Charlie the purpose of taking the trip to Manhattan: he plans to blow his savings on one last fling in the city, and then blow himself away with his service revolver. So when the blind man and his charge take a Ferrari for a test drive through a bizarrely deserted sector of Manhattan—with Frank behind the wheel—there is some momentary tension: will the old loon drive them both off a bridge? In fact, no—he's just after a life-affirming joyride.

Charlie thinks he's gotten through to the old man and convinced him to hand over all of his bullets. Then he walks in on Slade loading his gun. The boy tries to coax him into giving up his .45, but instead Frank points the gun at Charlie. Frank tells Charlie he's going to kill him in order to save him from having to decide what to do back at school on Monday. "I'm gonna kill you, boy," he warns, Pacino's voice crescendoing to an explosion on the phrase, "Because I can't bear the thought of you SELLING OUT!" After a long, increasingly tense and very shouty back-and-forth, during which Charlie repeatedly dares Frank to pull the trigger, Slade finally calls his bluff. Frank: You don't wanna die. Charlie: Neither do you. Frank: Give me one good reason not to. Charlie: I'll give you two: you can dance the tango and drive a Ferrari better than anyone I've ever seen.

Seduced by this vulnerable tyrant's lust for life, Charlie saves Frank through sheer force of admiration. In turn, Frank saves Charlie through sheer charisma. On Monday morning, Frank shows up at the disciplinary hearing at Charlie's school, and when Charlie is on the verge of being punished for refusing to rat out his classmates,

Frank launches into a speech in defense of the boy's integrity. In an echo of *...And Justice for All*, the headmaster tells Frank he's "out of order," to which he responds, "Out of order? I'll show you out of order. You don't know what out of order is. I'd show you, but I'm too old, I'm too tired, I'm too fucking blind. If I were the man I was five years ago, I'd take a FLAMETHROWER to this place! There was a time I could see. And I have seen. Boys like these, younger than these, their arms torn out, their legs ripped off. But there isn't nothin' like the sight of an amputated spirit... Fuck you, too!"

Incredibly, Frank's rambling, expletive-filled monologue embarrasses the headmaster enough that he agrees to let Charlie go without punishment, news that the assembled student body greets by exploding in cheers. Their respective crises resolved, the film ends with Frank returning to the Rossi home, greeting the Rossi children with affection. The suicidal head case has been transformed into a kindly old man, and the naïve boy has learned that moral compromise can be averted with a well-timed outburst.

Keeping It Real

Scent of a Woman's ludicrous happy ending confirms that the film takes place in a fantasy world, the antithesis of the realism (emotional, when not formal) Pacino was once associated with. And yet, as ever, the actor took pains to make the performance authentic.

He prepared for the part by spending time with members of the Associated Blind and the Lighthouse, two New York support organizations for the blind. He sought out patients who had lost their sight late in life, and talked to them about how it felt to no longer be able to see. "I would take a scene and act it out in the dark," Pacino said. "I would think about what it's like for a blind person to enter a room, how they would do the most simple, basic things." He added, "I don't think the blind are different from everyone else: some can cope, some cannot."[166]

Learning the physical aspect of the character, Pacino related, helped him with the mental part. "A ballet dancer spends all that time working on her movements, hours of labor, so when she jetés across the stage, she's not thinking of anything else but the power of the music around her and the story she's telling physically. You're trying to get yourself in a state where you're no longer thinking about what you're doing, but you've prepared yourself. And that's what improvisation really is."[167]

In order to get a sense of what Frank's life would have been like before the accident that robbed him of his sight, Pacino spent time with a lieutenant colonel who taught the actor about the practical habits of an army man. "We worked every day, and he'd teach me how to load and unload a .45 and all this stuff," Pacino remembered in 2007. "Every time I did something right, he'd go, 'Hoo-ah!' Finally, I asked, 'Where did you get that from?' And he said, 'When we were on the line, and you turned and snapped the rifle in the right way [you'd say], 'Hoo-ah!' So I just started doing it. It's funny where things come from. It wasn't in the script."[168]

An improvisation based on research, "Hoo-ah," would become as identifiable a catchphrase for Pacino as "Attica!"—and the contrast between the two highly repeatable phrases, one an extremely calculated political reference and the other a pre-verbal, guttural tic, says a lot about the differences between the Pacino of the 1970s and the Pacino of the 1990s. The former's work was so cerebral and internal that even when a character like Serpico had an outburst, some mystery remained regarding exactly what he was thinking and feeling. The Pacino of the 1990s was far less mysterious. He embroidered a character's inner life on the outside, on his face, in his body language, and, most notably, in his wildly dynamic voice.

Interestingly, it was the purely external nature of the performance, the almost hyperreal wearing of angst on the sleeve, that attracted the most ardent praise. In a rave review, Peter Rainer conceded that the film's climax was "cornball. But at least it's *rousingly* cornball. It's like watching the acting out of a dream revenge fantasy. Pacino works inside that dream with amazing grace."[169]

"In the past few years, Pacino, who used to be tight and withdrawn, has been opening himself up and putting more and more of himself on the screen," wrote David Denby in *New York* magazine. "In *Scent of a Woman* he offers the largest, most theatrical and emotional performance of his movie career."[170]

Why was "largest" used as an adjective of praise in regard to *Scent of a Woman*, when not even ten years earlier, the grandness of Pacino's performance in *Scarface* was widely criticized? Both performances require major physical transformations, while at the same time leaving room for Pacino the star to shine through. The difference between the two films is that *Scarface* is a massive middle finger to the American traditions of consumption and capitalism, as well as a Brechtian satire of one of the most popular Hollywood genres, the gangster film. Like *Scarecrow* before it, *Scarface* forced its audience to think about the dark underbelly of beloved tropes. It's a fantasy, but one that tells unpleasant truths. *Scent of a Woman*'s "dream revenge fantasy" is—no pun intended—blind to the real world.

The sheer mediocrity of the film helped Pacino's performance to stand out. *Scent of a Woman* was, as *New Yorker* critic Terrence Rafferty put it, "designed to be a holiday-season heart-warmer—one of those movies (like *Rain Man*, say) in which adventures are had by mismatched characters, laughs and tears are jerked from the defenseless audience, and lessons are learned by all." It fails

at this aim because Pacino's performance, Rafferty wrote, "taps emotions too complex and too frightening to be resolved by the simple moral victory that ends the picture...This is acting that chills the heart beyond any possibility of warming." And yet, its final act goes too far. "Too long, too loud: we sense that the filmmakers, weary pros, are faking a climax."[171]

Manufacturing Success

There are a couple of anecdotes about *Scent of a Woman*'s development and release that underline just how different this film was production-wise from those of the 1970s with which Pacino is most identified. For one thing, it's notable that the actor only made the movie to begin with because his agent talked him into it.

As Pacino would admit in his Oscar acceptance speech, his CAA agent Rick Nicita "urged me to do this part and actually threatened me if I didn't do it, 'cause I didn't want to do the part for some reason." According to Nicita, Pacino had initially passed because he felt the character of Slade "was tough to connect to... and he didn't have a military background." "The primary job of the agent is to advise clients," Nicita said. He was persistent in urging this client to take this film because to him "the character had the potential explosiveness and unpredictability that was perfect for Al."[172]

Pacino's career had recently been revived by *Sea of Love* and *Dick Tracy*, both box-office hits that earned the actor critical acclaim (and an Oscar nomination, for the latter). After the wilderness years of the 1980s, Pacino was back, and primed to take on a role that, like his great films of the 1970s, would combine character virtuosity with audience-pleasing entertainment. (Again, Pacino would have to weather accusations of following in the footsteps of Dustin Hoffman, who had rebounded from the disastrous *Ishtar* by playing a disabled man in *Rain Man*—and winning an Oscar for it.)

But audiences, and movies, had changed. When *Time Out London*'s Steve Grant referred to *Scent of a Woman* as "a touching but rather predictable and very caring 90s film,"[173] the reference to the just-beginning decade spoke volumes about what *Scent of a Woman* was not. The American cinema of the 1970s with which Pacino had made his name was rarely touching or predictable; it was, in fact, often predicated on a lack of sentimentality and an interest in defying established formulas of classical narrative cinema.

Pacino was no longer a brash young turk helping to invent a brave new world. He was now a decidedly middle-aged man who had openly returned to moviemaking after having gone broke trying to find himself through artistic endeavors. The period of his first flush of success, in which creative searching and popular entertainment routinely found purchase in the same movies, was

Opposite: Slade and Charlie take a blind joyride.

Retired from the army, blind, and feeling useless, Slade becomes suicidal.

long in the rearview. *The Godfather* had been the highest-grossing film of 1972. The highest-grossing film of 1992 was Disney's *Aladdin*. When *Scent of a Woman* went into production in late 1991, America was emerging from the first Gulf War, and the world was responding to the end of the Cold War and the triumph of capitalism it represented. When the film was released a year later, Bill Clinton was on the verge of inauguration. *Scent of a Woman* was nothing if not of its time: both touchy-feely and vulgar, a savvy commercial product masquerading as a pulse-taker of the human condition—the ultimate Clinton-era Hollywood production.

And *Scent of a Woman*'s marketing and distribution was nothing if not calculated. The *Los Angeles Times* reported that the final cut of the film was determined by test audiences. Martin Brest's director's cut came in at 160 minutes. Before the film's release, Universal showed test audiences increasingly shorter cuts of the film, according to marketing executive Perry Katz, "to see what we could lose and still have the picture work. Every movie has a fighting weight. If it's any longer, it's laborious. If it's any shorter, it's disjointed." At some point, it became evident that too much had been taken away, so the studio started adding material back. The 157-minute version was released because it ranked the highest with the focus groups.[174]

Oscar campaigning was another aspect of the industry that had changed since Pacino's heyday.

"With the Oscars, the only thing that bothers me is feeling like you're a loser, when you're really not," Pacino said in 1983. "You've been honored by being nominated. But I remember when I was there for *Serpico*, I thought I might have a chance. Then afterward there was this sense of feeling as though you lost. It's the way it's set up."

But this time, Pacino had some of the people who "set up" the system on his side. *Scent* was the first film Universal ever screened for Academy members before its commercial release—a savvy, ahead-of-its-time move that successfully cast Pacino's nomination and eventual win for Best Actor as an inevitability.[175]

Pacino finally did win his Oscar on March 29, 1993, twenty years after his first nomination. The award was presented by Jodie Foster; when Pacino, dressed in a bizarrely oversize tuxedo, made it to the stage, he was given a lengthy standing ovation. He spoke for just over three minutes, from a prepared page of notes pulled from his pocket, which he nervously held down to the podium with two fidgeting hands. He thanked O'Donnell, Brest, and screenwriter Bo Goldman; friends Ira Lewis, Lee Strasberg, and Charlie Laughton; executives at Universal Pictures and his agent. Then, at the end of the speech, he told an anecdote about having been approached by a fan and told that his success, as a kid who came from the South Bronx and evolved into one of the world's biggest stars, had been encouraging to her. Pacino took both hands

and gripped the Oscar trophy, lifting it off the podium and bringing it close to his heart. "So this is really a proud and hopeful moment for me, because I want to thank the Academy for giving us a gift of encouragement," Pacino said, his voice beginning to crack ever so slightly. "And this is a gift, a great gift to me. I thank you all, really."

Any actor's Oscar acceptance speech is likely both a genuine show of organic emotion and a calculated performance. In Pacino's case, he used his time on stage to remind the audience of his own origin legend, the long road to legitimacy, by paying his respects to the people who made his initial success possible, as well as the powerful industry players with whose help he had finally climbed the mountain of institutional commendation that had for so long eluded him. But while he undoubtedly revealed true feeling, he also was hardly naïve about the role the Oscars play in Hollywood's business machine.

"I was surprised how I felt after that. There was a kind of glow that lasted a couple of weeks. I'd never had that feeling," Pacino admitted three years later. "It's kind of like winning an Olympic medal, because it is so identifiable. Only in the Olympics you win it because you're the best— with the Oscar that's not necessarily the case," he added, with the wisdom of an eight-time loser. "It's just your turn."[176]

Pacino's turn came years, even decades, after his 1970s contemporaries—Beatty, Hoffman,

De Niro, Nicholson—had theirs. But to suggest that the matter of Pacino's legacy had been an open question to which *Scent of a Woman* had moved the Academy to finally add punctuation is to give Brest's film far too much credit. When Marlon Brando was nominated (and won) Best Actor for *The Godfather*, Pacino privately fumed that he, who was nominated (and lost) for Best Supporting Actor, had been gypped, given his greater amount of screen time, and the fact that the film's narrative arc is wedded to the long, slow transformation of Michael Corleone. But Brando had gone nearly twenty years without winning, and with *The Godfather*, he broke his own long streak of unprofitable projects. He was "due" in the sense that his body of work had gone long enough without celebration, and also, in the eyes of Hollywood's establishment, he deserved the award as an acknowledgment of what he had done for them lately. The same kind of Oscar accounting that Pacino felt had hurt him two decades earlier played to his favor in 1992. Given that Frank Slade is not a key presence in Brest's film until near the end of the two-hour thirty-seven minute movie's first act, Pacino's performance is arguably more supporting than lead, and yet he won Best Actor. Even more than Brando, Pacino was in essence being honored for his entire filmography, as well as a recently demonstrated willingness to play his part in the business of filmmaking.

On March 29, 1993, at the Dorothy Chandler Pavilion in Los Angeles, Al Pacino accepted the Academy Award for Best Actor in a Leading Role for his performance in Scent of a Woman. *After receiving a standing ovation from the audience, he gave the following three-minute speech:*

"You broke my streak. The last... I was at an affair recently—thank you so much for this by the way—I was at a ceremonial-type thing like this recently, and I didn't have a speech. I kept going into my pocket for a speech, but I never wrote one. But now I got one. It's here, and I should have had a little water before I got on because my mouth's dry.

"But I thank you and I just have to say... First, I don't know where he is in the house, I can't pick him out, but I got to thank him. I'm completely indebted to Marty Brest who directed the picture and who had such great love for this character I played. And that love is what he communicated to me every day, so I thank you, Marty, for that. I thank Bo Goldman, who wrote such a complicated, interesting, funny guy that could be and would be any actor's dream part. That part was so great. I thank Chris O'Donnell, my costar in this. He made every day a pleasure for me. And I thank the wonderful support of cast and crew, of course. I also want to thank Tom Pollock and Casey Silver at Universal Pictures, and my agent, Rick Nicita, who urged me to do this part and actually threatened me if I didn't do it, 'cause I didn't want to do the part for some reason. Ira Lewis, my friend and my colleague, who helped me, Ira Lewis. And the Associated Blind for their generous support to me.

"If you'll indulge me for a minute—I'm just not used to this, so I had to write this down. I had this thought, and I thought if I ever got up here I would say it. I've been very lucky. I found desire for what I do early in my life and I'm lucky because I had people who encouraged that desire, from Lee Strasberg, to my great friend and mentor Charlie Laughton, to the great writers and filmmakers that I've been fortunate enough to work with.

"Now, recently a young girl came up to me. I was at a function for the South Bronx, which is where I'm from. And she said that I had encouraged her, and that's not necessarily by my work but just by the fact that we came from the same place. And I just can't forget that girl, and I can't forget the kids out there who may be thinking tonight that if he can do it, I can do it. So this is really a proud and hopeful moment for me, because I want to thank the Academy for giving us a gift of encouragement. And this is a gift, a great gift to me. I thank you all, really. Thank you."

9

Vincent Hanna

Heat (1995)
Michael Mann

"I've got to hold on to my angst. I need it.
It keeps me sharp. On the edge. Where I gotta be."
—Vincent Hanna

Released in late 1995, Michael Mann's *Heat* is a study of warring dualities: criminal versus cop, man versus woman, home life versus street life, dreams versus reality, internal versus external. Animating this study of mirror opposites are Al Pacino and Robert De Niro, two actors whose careers had long been linked, even though, up to this point, they had never shared a scene on film. As critic Roger Ebert wrote, there was great significance to these two actors teaming up to make this film, at this time: "De Niro and Pacino, veterans of so many great films in the crime genre, have by now spent more time playing cops and thieves than most cops and thieves have. There is always talk about how actors study people to base their characters on. At this point in their careers, if Pacino and De Niro go out to study a cop or a robber, it's likely their subject will have modeled himself on their performances in old movies."[177]

The film tracks the intertwined paths of De Niro's Neil McCauley—a master thief who heads a crew specializing in stealth, multimillion-dollar scores—and Pacino's Vincent Hanna, a weary robbery/homicide detective whose obsession with catching crooks like McCauley has already destroyed two marriages and is eating away at a third. When we meet him, it's early morning, and Hanna is still in bed, making love to his gorgeous, somewhat younger wife, Justine (Diane Venora). Hanna's morning routine constitutes the film's third scene: we've already seen McCauley and his crony Chris Shiherlis (Val Kilmer) lay groundwork for an armored-car robbery, which Hanna will later investigate. That Hanna's sleeping with his wife when the crime he'll spend the film investigating (to the detriment of his marriage) first begins suggests equally his relative lack of power—he's lagging behind his prey before he even gets out of bed—and that it's impossible to function simultaneously as a husband and as a professional in the world he works in.

A cat-and-mouse game ensues, with Hanna and his fellow detectives always a step behind McCauley and crew even after locking them into total surveillance. Hanna openly admires McCauley's talent—"drop of the hat, these guys were rock 'n' roll", the cop compliments the crook—which is notable because the detective seems to have so little interest in human relations. Think of his deadpan mini-monologue when he walks in on his wife making breakfast for "Ralph," a stranger with whom she obviously spent the night: "I'm angry. I'm very angry, Ralph. You know, you can ball my wife if she wants you to. You can lounge around here on her sofa, in her ex-husband's dead-tech, post-modernistic bullshit house if you want to. But you do not get to watch my fucking television set!" By this point—twenty-three years after the masterpiece of internalization that was Pacino's performance in *The Godfather*—we all know that when Al Pacino is playing an angry man, the last way we're going to learn that is through his literal dialogue.

True Romance

While *Heat* is, on its surface, about men juggling contradictory commitments to work and women, the true romance of the film is between Pacino's character and De Niro's, the only genuine love scene their sole face-to-face meeting in a coffee shop. In this incredible scene, the two men find that they have a lot of common ground: their inability to maintain domestic relationships, their obsessive burrowing into their work, and their certainty that even after this bonding session, each is prepared to kill the other to save his own hide.

McCauley lives by one rule: never get "attached to anything you are not willing to walk out on in thirty seconds flat if you feel the heat around the corner." Vincent has tried, over and over again, to maintain a "regular" life, a charade that inevitably crumbles as, night after night, he prowls the streets hunting bad guys. Mann often sets De Niro against a background of cerulean blue—intense, but cool—while Pacino's image is accented with red: neon red, bloodred, the color of the "heat" he embodies to McCauley, and of his burning-ember personality.

The difference in the two approaches to life is manifested in the actors' appearances. Essentially the same age—Pacino was fifty-five when the film was released, while De Niro was fifty-two—they seem, on screen in this film, to occupy opposite

ends of what could be reasonably defined as
"middle age." De Niro appears to be holding on to
youth, if just barely; he dresses like a man of
achievement, in slick silvery suits and crisp white
shirts, but his face is too smooth and fresh. There
is no sign of all the character has been through—
stints in prison, likely no shortage of narrow
escapes from death—in the even, economic way
he speaks, or in his almost lazy eyes.

By contrast, Pacino's Vincent Hanna is a
broadly sketched cartoon of what stress can do to
a man's physical appearance. The Oscar Wilde–
loving Pacino might have thought of Hanna as the
walking painting of decay trailing McCauley's
suspiciously youthful Dorian Gray. Hanna's suits
are darker than McCauley's, and they hang off
Pacino's diminutive, lurched-forward frame.
The beleaguered detective is several times aligned
with the corpses on whose behalf he profession-
ally seeks retribution. Justine complains, "You
don't live with me, you live among the remains
of dead people," and for much of the film, Pacino
seems to embody the "big black balloon people"
with "eight-ball eyes" he says he has recurring
nightmares about—the walking dead.

Heat ends with Hanna—the cop, ostensibly
the good guy—killing McCauley—the criminal,
a thief and murderer, by standard definitions a
bad guy. The tragedy of the film is that McCauley
has been shot down because he couldn't resist one
last act of revenge before embracing a "regular"

life for the first time, while Hanna—for whom
death, at this point, would seem to be a relief—
is left standing to plod through his graveyard
of a life. Perhaps in recognition of this irony—
or maybe just out of respect for his dying
adversary, his mirror image on the other side of
the legal divide—Hanna grasps McCauley's hand
as he passes. In the film's final shot, the dying
McCauley and the living Hanna, facing opposite
directions, form a tableau that resembles a
yin-yang symbol—their differences
complementary to the end.

A Core of Realism

Heat is a combination of realism and myth—
as familiar a duality to Pacino as playing a
lawman who feels a commonality with a criminal.

Before Mann became known as the stylish
auteur of *Miami Vice*, he trained in nonfiction
filmmaking in Britain, and his first feature, the
made-for-TV movie *The Jericho Mile* (1979), was
shot at California's Folsom Prison, with actors
from the outside interacting with real prisoners
in speaking parts. "People want reality in movies
today," Mann said in 1981. "They want the real
thing, real people, real locations. They see the
real thing on their television news shows. They
want a movie to look real."[178]

As Nick James notes, Mann's interest in realism
remains constant throughout his filmography,

even as, stylistically, the films seem to become more plastic—which forces the viewer to think about where they get their idea of what "realism" looks and feels like. "In the UK, we tend to think of grainy, television-scale dramas about social ills as our touchstone of realism. For Mann it is more about getting authentic physical and psychological detail right and ripe for its blowing up into mainstream entertainment."[179]

Heat was shot entirely in real Los Angeles locations—no studios or soundstages were used—including the streets of the downtown financial district, the Los Angeles International Airport, and a working bank and open hospital. In 1995, the city was still recovering from the Rodney King beating and the subsequent 1992 LA riots, as well as the O.J. Simpson freeway chase and trial. Images of the city's streets serving as a canvas for real-life crime, punishment, and social unrest had recently been broadcast internationally. This gave the real locations seen in the film a kind of extratextual tension.

Then there was the true story that planted the seed of the film. Mann had a friend, Chuck Adamson, who, as a cop in Chicago in the 1960s, had chased and ultimately killed the real Neil McCauley. "What was most striking was that he'd met McCauley; quite by accident, they'd had coffee together. And Chuck had respected the guy's professionalism—he was a really good thief, which is exciting to a detective... Chuck

was going through some crisis in his life, and they wound up having one of those intimate conversations you sometimes have with strangers. There was a real rapport between them; yet both men verbally recognized one would probably kill the other... But it was the intimacy, the mutual rapport that became the nucleus of the film."[180]

Two Different Methods

Like the men they played in *Heat*, Pacino and De Niro had a rapport, but the demands of their job had previously kept them away from each other. And there were key philosophical differences, too.

De Niro and Pacino first became friends in the mid-1960s, when both were studying acting in New York City. Sally Kirkland, a friend of Pacino and former girlfriend of De Niro, remembers that the two actors spent time together at the Actors Studio, even though De Niro was not officially a member. "Al and Bobby were in the same room a lot. They became friends, and there was a healthy kind of competition between them—if one of them got high marks, the other would work all the harder to be great in their next project. Al would watch Bobby and Bobby would watch Al."[181]

As they moved through the ranks of the New York theater world, and then graduated to Hollywood stardom, Pacino and De Niro both came to represent a certain authenticity in performance style and appearance. But Pacino's

and De Niro's approaches to "realistic" acting came from different places. Actors Studio student Pacino was a faithful follower of Lee Strasberg and his version of the Stanislavski Method (although the teacher didn't like the use of the word "method"). Strasberg advocated "emotional recall," meaning that actors were asked to build characters based on their own experiences and remembered feelings, drawing from within in order to create the sense of a character whose life began before the beginning of the narrative in question and would continue after. De Niro, meanwhile, studied with Strasberg's rival, Stella Adler, whose interpretation of Stanislavski's teachings disregarded an actor's personal history, and focused on external stimuli to conjure the character, rather than building it out of the performer's personal internal material. De Niro once said, "Acting is not about playing on your neuroses. It's about the character, being faithful to the text, the script. Not going on about it as if it was all about you."[182]

Mann noticed the contrast in performance style on the set of *Heat*. De Niro, the director said, "sees the part as a construction, working incredibly hard, detail by detail, bit by bit building character, as if he were I. M. Pei. The way Al acquires insight into character is different. It's more like Picasso staring at an empty canvas for many hours in intense concentration. And then there's a series of brush strokes. And a piece of the character is alive."[183]

To help get Pacino into character, Mann said, "There was somebody I wanted him to meet— I based Al's character in the movie on this guy. When Al finally met the guy, within five minutes, he got him and he got everything I'd been saying about him. And I don't mean that he copied his mannerisms or gestures. I mean he captured the most profound sense of the man—just like that. It took me years to get what Al got in a few minutes." "If you have a chance to meet somebody who can help you, you do it," Pacino acknowledged. "Now you'd think that I'd know all about playing detectives, since I've been playing them all my life, since way back in *Serpico*. But I don't remember, so I had to meet with a few people. I didn't do much research. It was nothing special, really."[184]

In the 1970s, Pacino sometimes fell so deep into character that he had trouble coming out— as he marveled about the time he found himself giving a friend legal advice while playing a lawyer. But as time went on, he no longer felt that such total immersion was necessary. "When I was younger, making films, I would try to stay in the role and be in a state of isolation, both on and off set," he said. 'If I were to go back, I would tell myself: 'You don't have to do that all the time, Al. Just be yourself, and only when it's time to act, only then get into the role.'"[185]

As Hanna, Pacino speaks loudly, barking and bellowing in an exaggerated hipster patois that

Heat made movie history by uniting Pacino and Robert De Niro in the same film frame. In 2008, when director Jon Avnet tried to repeat that trick for the buddy cop film Righteous Kill, *the bloom was off the rose: all involved were accused of chasing a paycheck.* Newsweek *suggested that fans go back and rewatch* Heat *instead.*

"Once upon a time, the prospect of Robert De Niro and Al Pacino on screen together, mano a mano, would've provoked a wildly different reaction than the one I have whenever I see posters for their new cop flick, *Righteous Kill.* Twenty years ago I'd have raced you to the theater. Now? All I see is two bored, scowling men paired up for a movie that sounds as though it's about a surfing competition ('Dude, that was a righteous kill!'), and all I think is, 'Oh, no.'

This isn't the first time De Niro and Pacino have stooped to self-parody in paycheck roles. It's just the first time they've done it as a team... My advice: skip *Righteous Kill* and catch De Niro and Pacino together at a moment when 'De Niro and Pacino together' actually meant something. It happened only once, in Michael Mann's 1995 crime epic *Heat*... In Mann's meticulously constructed saga, there's no earthly reason for the good guy and the bad guy to meet for a chat, except to give the audience this moment of bliss. Once De Niro and Pacino are across the table from each other, the movie drops away, as if Mann pressed 'pause,' and the two characters discuss who they are and why they do the things they do, like rival samurai trading philosophies during a breather from

combat. De Niro's bank robber is wary but calm and guileless; Pacino's cop is a cocksure raconteur, savoring the presence of a worthy adversary. There's no music, no plot, no fancy camera tricks. Just six minutes of pure acting. The men finish their coffee, then return to their separate worlds. If De Niro and Pacino had any sense— any fingertips for the meta-universe of movies, where such collisions are so powerful precisely because they're so rare—they would've left it that way."[r]

Al Pacino's performance
is a highly calculated inflation
of the character's inability
to live on the same plane as
those around him.

he punctuates by snapping his fingers in between phrases. "I've got to hold on to my angst," he tells Justine, as an excuse for why he can't communicate with her. "I need it." Snap. "It keeps me sharp." Snap. "On the edge." Snap. "Where I gotta be." Even when he's not keeping the beat between phrases with his fingers, Pacino's vocal cadences in *Heat* bring Pacino's musical tendencies to the forefront: in one interrogation, he literally bursts into song as a show of disrespect for the informant he's grilling. The lines Pacino sings, from the Jimmy Webb tune "By the Time I Get to Phoenix," are not in Mann's screenplay; the actor embellished much of his dialogue through on-set improvisation.

"Al really likes to play around," remembered costar Hank Azaria, whose one scene with Pacino in *Heat* includes one of the actor's most memorably inflated line readings. "I say something like, I don't know why I got mixed up with this stupid broad, and he says... 'Cause she's got a great ass!' He just screams it. And that was the line, but Al kind of yelled it for the first time, and he did it so completely out of nowhere that it scared me. So much so that I just went, 'Jesus!' Not in character, just as Hank... And then Al improvised, 'I'm sorry. Something happens to me when I think about a woman's ass.' Or whatever it is that he said. And that actually made it into the movie!"[186]

One thing from Mann's script that didn't make it into the movie: a single scene of Pacino's character snorting cocaine, which the actor later said had been his impetus for the character's odd rhythm and sudden explosions. "I based my character on the fact that he chipped cocaine, so my interpretation—my reactions to things—were colored by that. It's like, 'What's that guy so nervous about?'"[187] This may explain why some of Pacino's line readings are so heightened. It's almost as though he's treating the dialogue as if it's in quotes: when Hanna offers his invitation to McCauley ("Whaddya say I buy you a cuppa coffee?"), it really feels as though Pacino is stepping out of character to tell the audience, "Here's what you've been waiting for!"

When it came time to film that centerpiece coffee date, there was no improvisation. "In *Heat*, for the scene with Robert De Niro and me, that was completely scripted," Pacino said in 2007. "There were no rehearsals. I just met him there."[188] "I never wanted them to rehearse," Mann said. "I didn't want to miss a millisecond of Al reacting off Bob. A small gesture on Al's face would bounce to Bob, who would put his hand on the table. It went on and on."[189] Mann said he shot thirteen takes of the scene, uninterrupted, "because I wanted the organic unity of a single performance. I just sat them across the table from each other and shot with two cameras simultaneously, which is very difficult on widescreen, and hard to light. And what you see is nearly all the eleventh take; I knew—we all knew—we'd got it on the ninth, but take eleven had some extra special qualities, little harmonics."[190]

Mann never frames the face of both actors in the same shot; the entire conversation is edited in the shot-reverse-shot style, the back of one man's head visible when we're looking at the other's face. This enhances the mirror symbolism of the scene—for both the characters and the actors who play them. The clear meta-subtext of the scene, a time out for rivals to admit their mutual appreciation and dependency on their opposite/twin, is a reenactment of Sally Kirkland's observation as to what happens when these guys get in the same room: "Al would watch Bobby and Bobby would watch Al."[191]

New Hollywood's Descendant

Pacino—icon of 1970s New Hollywood, who retreated from an even newer Hollywood as the industry and the audience transformed in the 1980s, only to be celebrated in the early 1990s for playing nice with Hollywood's capitalist demands—is the perfect actor to embody what Steven Rybin calls the "predicament" of Mann's creative project within a highly commercial system. In that Mann's films "aspire to greatness and significance," Rybin writes, "they suggest... that the end of the period we now know historically as the New Hollywood did not spell the ending of meaningful filmmaking in the industry."[192]

It was a sentiment with which Pacino himself disagreed. "The problem is that films just aren't as good as they were in the 1970s. Filmmakers are afraid to address anything. Oliver Stone is the exception. I think it's too much about marketing these days," he said while promoting *Heat*.[193] But, of course, *Heat* itself was an auteur film commercially justified by the marketing opportunity presented by the pairing of the two stars.

Heat wasn't a blockbuster, but its $67 million gross was slightly more than *Scent of a Woman*'s, making it Pacino's most-seen film since *Dick Tracy*. But the film was ignored by Academy voters. While many critics raved, particularly about the performances, others were turned off by what they judged as self-indulgent pretension. "Here's a great two-hour movie heedlessly inflated by existentialist gases," sniffed Joe Morgenstern in the *Wall Street Journal*.[194]

As we've seen, by the mid-1990s, Pacino had turned in several performances that courted self-parody; in fact, some critics essentially started accusing him of playing "Al Pacino" as soon as they gave up comparing him to Dustin Hoffman. *Heat* gave critics a new opportunity to accuse Pacino of falling into autopilot. Ironically, critics of Pacino seemed generally as nostalgic for the 1970s as Pacino admitted he himself was. "What happened to Al Pacino?" Rex Reed wrote shortly after *Heat*'s release. "When he began

his acting career, we thought he was Brando, James Dean, and Monty Clift all rolled into one, with a Bronx accent. Now his eyes alone do the acting for him—they're like black olives rolling around in buttermilk, and there's something heavy and fixed about them, almost dazed."[195]

Arguably, this is exactly what Pacino was going for in *Heat*—Reed's description seems to unwittingly echo Hanna's description of the corpses in his dreams. It's harder to argue with critic Dyland Jones's assertion that "Pacino seems to act like a method pimp. His most annoying trait is speaking very softly and then suddenly SCREAMING or YELPING a random word or two before returning to a whisper."[196]

That's not an inaccurate description of any number of Pacino performances. However, his performance in *Heat* is not mere calcified shtick or over-the-top winking; it's a highly calculated inflation of the character's inability to live on the same plane with those around him. It's often funny, but it's also tragic, and its core is the coffee shop scene, in which both men let down their defenses, and Pacino reveals Hanna to be simultaneously terrified and also ready and willing to inflict terror to protect himself—in other words, an authentic divided human being.

Over the next fifteen years, Pacino would mount a number of labors of love in protest of the tyranny of marketing he railed against— *Looking for Richard*, *The Merchant of Venice*,

the fiction/documentary hybrid *Wilde Salomé*. In his for-hire work, he seemed to gravitate toward the highly marketable, whether it be stunts (*Angels in America* [2005], *You Don't Know Jack* [2010], the comic villain of *Ocean's Thirteen* [2007]) or lawmen and crook characters he could seemingly act on autopilot (*The Recruit* [2003], *Insomnia* [2002], *Righteous Kill* [2008]). And then, finally, he'd make a film that would take on the construct of marketing-dictated content head-on—and he'd suffer the consequences.

10

"Al Pacino"

Jack and Jill (2011)
Dennis Dugan

"When I look at her, I see me. I see what I was. I'm lost."
— "Al Pacino"

In February 2011, the New York City repertory theater Film Forum mounted a series called "Pacino's 70s," consisting of seven films from that decade (*The Panic in Needle Park*, *Scarecrow*, both *Godfather*s, *Serpico*, *Dog Day Afternoon*, and *...And Justice for All*). The comprehensive-sounding title of the series was slightly misleading: all but one of these films (*Justice*) was made between 1971 and 1975. Several local film writers used the event as an opportunity to measure how much has changed in the many decades since these films were made.

"If I were bitchy, I'd subtitle [the series] *When He Was Great*," wrote David Edelstein in *New York* magazine. "Okay, he has been brilliant since, but always high on the hog, which isn't the case in his breakthrough as Michael in *The Godfather* and its first sequel—internal, amazingly controlled performances."[197]

In the *New York Times*, Stephen Holden's consideration of the evolution of Pacino's stardom called to mind the old aphorism from *Sunset Boulevard*: it was the pictures that got small. "His acting gift is magnificently intact. It may be too large for Hollywood movies whose artistic reach has diminished since the 1970s."[198]

Nine months later, audiences and critics would see Al Pacino in a role that not only showcased his very particular "gifts" but skewered them. *Jack and Jill*, released in the fall of 2011, is a crass family comedy in which Adam Sandler plays the two title roles—Jack, a wealthy Beverly Hills advertising executive, and his well-meaning but socially dysfunctional twin sister, Jill, who comes to visit him from the Bronx, where Jack and Jill grew up—and Al Pacino plays "Al Pacino," a famous actor, also from the Bronx, who is in the midst of a midlife identity and career crisis, and becomes convinced that a romance with hometown girl Jill will help him find himself. *Jack and Jill* was savaged by critics and, for an Adam Sandler comedy, it underperformed at the box office. Some singled out Pacino's decision to participate as a sign that the seventy-one-year-old actor had lost touch with reality. "This is now the official low point of a great career," wrote

online film critic Drew McWeeny, "a moment so relentlessly weird and ill-considered that I'm wondering if someone should be given power of attorney over him to prevent him from further ruining his good name."[199]

Jack and Jill may not be a great film—it may not even be a good film—but while Pacino's role within it is certainly "relentlessly weird," to call it "ill-considered" is to diminish Pacino's abundantly evident self-knowledge and to ignore his pattern of proving to be the auteur, the guiding creative force, of his own career. Pacino's "Al Pacino" is nothing if not a direct and public attempt on the part of the actor to confront his image—as a representative of serious acting, as a symbol of the honesty and integrity of 1970s New Hollywood in contrast with the corporate cynicism of the current industry, and as a somewhat eccentric star—and the baggage that persona brings into the acting process. In mocking both Pacino's actual body of work and the sometimes skewed perceptions of him in popular culture, the film allows Pacino to playfully face criticisms that his best days are behind him while at the same time pointing back to the very earliest manifestation of his gift for physical comedy. As a child, Pacino concealed his social anxieties and ingratiated himself with his peers through playground pranks and imitations; *Jack and Jill* comes from the same instinctual place.

Subverting Stardom

Jack and Jill is the latest in a series of collaborations between comedian-turned-movie-star Adam Sandler and director Dennis Dugan. Since helming the Sandler vehicle *Happy Gilmore* in 1996, Dugan has made a living mounting films around the personalities of a crew of stand-up comedians who parlayed early-1990s stints on *Saturday Night Live* into movie careers. Of that crew, which includes David Spade, Rob Schneider, and the late Chris Farley, Sandler has by far been the most successful at maintaining a consistent persona that can be counted on to attract big box-office returns, largely through films directed by Dugan. *Jack and Jill*, written by Sandler and Steve Koren, was the comedian's seventh collaboration with Dugan, and second in 2011 alone, after *Just Go with It*, which like *Jack and*

A portrait of Al Pacino, 2004.

Jill featured an Oscar-winning serious actor (Nicole Kidman) in a supporting role.

Even as the basic premise requires Sandler to dress in drag and literally play against himself, *Jack and Jill* does not do much to challenge or critique the Sandler persona. Dugan has been so instrumental in shaping the notion of what constitutes an Adam Sandler movie as a lucrative subgenre of contemporary Hollywood comedy that you wouldn't expect him to make a film that does anything to question or subvert that format or Sandler's role in it. In fact, Sandler is an example of how futile it can be for a major star to attempt to confront his public persona within a movie: the critical and commercial failure of Judd Apatow's self-reflexive Sandler vehicle *Funny People* apparently reinforced Sandler's personal autopilot by punishing him for trying to step outside of it.

Pacino was downplayed in the marketing campaign for *Jack and Jill*, which centered on Sandler's cross-dressing dual performance and gave the impression that the elder actor's presence would be reduced to that of a large cameo. The great, happy surprise of the film is that the gimmick central to Sandler's performance, and the meta-concept dictating Pacino's, are not separate but fully integrated in a far-reaching exploration of identity and role-playing that both draws on Pacino's rich career and allows him to finally fulfill his long-repressed desire to show off his comic chops.

"I've always thought of myself as a clown. I love the circus, silent screen comedy, triple-takes," Pacino said in 1975. "So what do I get to play? Tough punks, drug addicts, underworld leaders... no clowns."[200] Nearly thirty years later, he still distinguished himself as a cutup—although now, he did so wistfully. "That's how I saw myself, in comedy," Pacino noted in 2004. "I didn't know I would do this with my life. I didn't know what the hell I was going to do." Citing *Dog Day Afternoon* as an example of a film in which he was able to use his body comedically, he continued, "That's where humor lives for me. In the body. The Steve Martin kind of stuff or Jim Carrey, that's what I like. I've always felt that's what I would like to do."[201]

It took him seven more years to find a role that would combine that kind of introspection about his life with this long-dormant ambition.

Professional Crises

Jack (Sandler) is a top advertising executive with a beautiful wife (Katie Holmes), two adorable kids, and a sprawling Los Angeles manse. At the beginning of the film, his exaggerated good fortune is threatened by two unfolding crises. He's been tasked by Dunkin' Donuts to seduce Al Pacino, an actor notoriously averse to lending his name and likeness to endorsements, into appearing in a television commercial for their new iced-coffee drink, the Dunkaccino.

Meanwhile, Jack's twin sister, Jill (also played by Sandler), a gregarious and suspiciously unfeminine New York spinster, is arriving for her annual stay at Jack's home for the holidays. Apparently never less than a handful, Jill is this year particularly tempestuous and emotionally chaotic, owing to her grief over the recent passing of their mother. Jack is the only family she has left, and her loneliness and neediness lead her to contrive to extend her stay.

Loud, overbearing, and hirsute, with a thick, high-pitched New York accent, Jill is an inflated stereotype of a matronly Jewish-American woman. Jack's evident embarrassment in regard to his sister seems to have less to do with her oversize personality—which Jack's wife and kids alternately overlook and embrace as charming—than with Jack's apparent desire to erase his humble roots in the working-class, immigrant-heavy New York borough of the Bronx, to better fit into the role of a power player in the superficial new money world of Los Angeles.

We're meant to understand before we even meet his character that "Pacino" is going to be a tough get for Jack's commercial, because his life and career are based on integrity—a value that Jack, and the industry he's part of, look down on as a quaint or old-fashioned obstacle to the inevitability of commerce. The question of "selling out" reverberates throughout *Jack and Jill* on both a narrative level and as meta-text. Pacino's very participation in the movie could be (and was, by many journalists) considered a sellout, and an unusually blatant one; the text of the film itself seems to roll its eyes at anyone high and mighty enough to act as though a sellout, in today's corporate culture, is still anathema. Indeed, it was interesting to see third parties suggest that Pacino should feel shame for taking the part, when Pacino himself has historically been incredibly open about the compromises inherent in maintaining his lifestyle—he's always contextualized his initial return to the screen after his mid-1980s hiatus as compelled by a need to pay bills—as well as the fact that even he, one of our greatest living actors, cannot always pay those bills by making quality pictures. "The worse the script is, the more money you're offered," he said in 2007. "Show me a bad script, and I will show you a big payday. Conversely, show me a really great script and forget it. You're lucky if you don't have to pay for it."[202] As far as paydays go, it's hard to see how this one is particularly egregious, when you consider that at least *Jack and Jill* has Pacino playfully confronting his image, where many of his films over the last two decades (from the much-maligned *Righteous Kill* to "quality" projects like *The Godfather Part III* and *Insomnia*) have simply asked him to rehearse it.

Jack and Jill reflexively plays with the notion that Pacino is at such a low point in his vaunted career that he might be willing to consider a blatant sellout move. Soon after Jack learns that his company's contract with Dunkin' Donuts is contingent on him landing Pacino for the advert, we see Jack watch a viral video titled "Al Pacino's Nervous Breakdown??" Shot from the seats of a Los Angeles theater where the Pacino character is starring in a run of *Richard III* (a role Pacino has taken pains to associate himself with, via his directorial effort *Looking for Richard*), it shows the actor reacting to a ringing cell phone by breaking character and throwing an angry tantrum. After bawling out the phone owner, he turns plaintive. "This has got to stop. I'm losing my mind. Help me. Where am I?" Framing Pacino's stardom and its emphasis on purity in the context of a celebrity tantrum, caught on tape and consumed for laughs, may be an attempt to draw in younger viewers unfamiliar with Pacino's glory days. But it also playfully suggests that the "Pacino" character is so far from his peak that maybe participating in a cheesy TV ad isn't totally outside the realm of possibility. The viral video is an exaggeration of an incident that really happened: a cell phone went off during a performance of *Oedipus* at the Actors Studio in 2002. The phone's owner, according to a witness, "was obviously so mortified that they didn't think to just turn the darn thing off. So when it went on beeping with the message alert, Mr. Pacino stopped and stared stone cold directly toward that person. What a look."[203] Here we see the Pacino crescendo theory in practice: in real life, Pacino showed his power through a silent response, while in fiction, he lost his cool. Knowing this allows us to read *Jack and Jill*'s portrayal of the Pacino mythology on the whole as an imaginary inflation of the real in which Pacino plays with a kind of worst-case-scenario version of himself.

The public perception of Pacino as a celebrity who is famous because of his humorless commitment to his craft is mocked in the scene in which "Pacino" and Jill first meet. Having learned that Pacino is scheduled to attend a basketball game, Jack gets tickets for himself and brings Jill in an effort to give his sister the "twin time" she's been begging for. Pacino indeed is in attendance at the basketball game, seated courtside next to Johnny Depp (also playing himself). Wearing a hat and a costume beard, he tells Depp, "I'm doing research. I don't want to be recognized." The next shot shows Depp and Pacino on the arena's monitors, having been caught by the "Celebrity Cam," Pacino's name blinking under the image of his poorly disguised face. At halftime, Jack approaches Pacino to introduce himself. The star tries to ignore the intrusion, until he spots Jill lurking behind her brother. There's a close-up on Pacino's face, a moment of realization. He murmurs to himself, "Dulcinea."

Pacino introduces himself, and Jill admits that she's not familiar with his films. "I hear you're

"Al Pacino" meets Jill at a Lakers game after his ludicrous disguise fails.

very serious," she comments. The actor shrugs. "Eh, you know." They bond over their common hometown. It's clear that Pacino is interested in getting to know Jill better. But Jill is oblivious, looking over Pacino's shoulder in hopes of spotting a 'real' celebrity like Ryan Seacrest. After Jack and Jill have returned to their seats (which place them amidst the rabble, far from Pacino), an usher delivers a gift for Jill from "Mr. Pacino": a hot dog with his phone number written in ketchup.

While Jack sees an opportunity to get close to Pacino for professional purposes via his sister, Jill tells her brother she has no interest in dating the star. (No matter how famous he is, at seventy-one, Pacino is at least old enough to be Jill's father.) And yet, a few scenes later when Pacino contrives to rescue Jill from an unsatisfying joint birthday party for her and Jack, she willingly follows him to his Beverly Hills mansion, where a personal chef prepares a smorgasbord of birthday desserts. Once Jill enters Pacino's home, *Jack and Jill* enters a thrillingly weird realm of Pacino send-up. The actor's real history (frequent references to his films and his paucity of Oscars) is blended with half-true perceptions (he quotes Stella Adler, when in real life Pacino studied the Method with Adler's rival, Lee Strasberg) and total fantasy to create a comic, alternate-universe version of a star in crisis, who becomes obsessed with his roots and can only move forward by facing and working through his past.

The film's smartest, funniest commentary on the real Pacino's struggles to earn recognition in Hollywood comes in this scene. Pacino presents fellow Bronx native Jill with a stickball bat he's held on to since childhood. Right there in the actor's study, Pacino invites his oddly muscular inamorata to practice her swing. She demurs, but he says, "Jill, it's in you. It's in your DNA! Just think 'Bronx.'" She swings at the first pitch, and hits a fly ball directly into the bookshelf, where it smashes and destroys Pacino's Oscar. "Oh, I'm so sorry!" Jill exclaims. "I'm sure you have others, though." Pacino looks stunned—not mad, but almost excited, as though the destruction of his Oscar gives him a fresh start. He says, "Uh, you'd think it, but oddly enough I don't. But I have you." She makes an excuse to leave, telling him she's still on New York time. "You know what time it is for me? It is time for my salvation," "Pacino" responds. "Because finally, I've found the one woman, with all her rough human charm, who will lead me back... to sanity!"

"Pacino" becomes obsessed with the notion that Jill is his key to finding his way back to the authenticity he once represented. Pacino the character acknowledges that he's in the midst of a crisis: he's been invited to play Don Quixote on Broadway, but he can't put his personal troubles aside to find the character. His anxiety comes out in a scene where he breaks into Jack's house looking for Jill. When he doesn't find her, he confesses to her brother, "When I look at her, I see me. I see what I was. I'm lost... Jill's gonna get me there." The attraction is based in large part on his perception of her as being "real," authentic to where they're both from and in contrast to the world of celebrity that he occupies. In the context of the movie, the joke is that Jill, of course, is not even a real woman—and that Pacino is so deluded he can't tell.

But that this is how Al Pacino the character's midlife crisis manifests itself is fitting, in that it points back to the qualities essential to Pacino's early stardom. If the difference in his build, ethnicity, voice, and approach all marked him as a "real person" in the 1970s, and thus established his stardom, it makes perfect sense that he'd be drawn to the same qualities while attempting to crawl out of the woods. Pacino has said he understood the character as "a guy who just wants to go back home, wants to be simple again, but will never be able to be that way again."[204] Within the real Pacino's filmography, *Jack and Jill* looks like an attempt to move forward by facing the chasm between who he currently is and who he used to be.

The skewed state of mind of "Al Pacino" is most spectacularly explicated in a scene set during a *Richard III* performance. Again, a cell phone rings in the middle of the show—but this time, it's Al's. It's Jack calling, and, still on stage, Pacino answers. Jack suggests that he'll arrange a date between Pacino and his sister if Pacino agrees to do the Dunkin' Donuts commercial. "Don't you know me?" Pacino asks, enraged. "Don't you know I would use all of my power to keep a commercial like that from happening?"

An audience member recognizes this line as a throwback to Pacino's roots. "Is he seriously breaking out *The Godfather II*?" The audience loves this "performance"; with Pacino still on the phone, they start chanting his name. The joke is that the actorly integrity that Pacino stands for is lost on an average fan. The masses don't care about his process or his evolving technique or the sanctity of the theater—they just want to hear his greatest hits. Here this "sellout" movie cogently critiques the mentality that leads a director to ask the actor to give him "more Pacino," that leads the star to take parts for which he is handsomely paid to recycle rather than innovate, and that ultimately leads to the complaint that Pacino is on autopilot. Autopilot, *Jack and Jill* suggests, is exactly what the paying public wants from its stars; they want performers to be reliable, familiar commodities. It follows that perhaps one of the reasons why *Jack and Jill* failed so miserably is that by confronting his persona through comedy, Pacino was deviating from the hard-ass, humorless characters he's best known for. "I love the idea of playing an older movie star, clinging, trying to get back to what it was that made him

do this thing in the first place," Pacino said of his character. "And no matter how crazy he is, his instincts are still working as an actor... This is the actor's journey out of madness."

For "Al Pacino," the goal of that journey is to use his personal life to figure out how to play Don Quixote in a production of *Man of La Mancha*. The film's press notes left it to Pacino—for whom participation in marketing materials was rare—to unpack the *Man of La Mancha* references running through the film: "In *Man of La Mancha*, Don Quixote is a madman who believes himself to be a knight, and he believes Dulcinea to be a princess, even though she's an ugly peasant. He falls madly in love with her by endowing her with virtues she doesn't really possess. When my character meets Jill, he does the same thing. She becomes his Dulcinea. In a sense, my character unconsciously uses her as a tool to find out if he indeed wants to play the part of Don Quixote. He gives Jill all the traits of the character Dulcinea so he can rehearse it, try it out, and see if it fits. He doesn't even know he's doing it, but there's method in his madness."[205]

The method is the Method: by courting Jill, "Pacino" is using real life as a kind of sandbox, re-creating Don Quixote's situation in order to give himself lived experience that he can bring into the performance. In terms of an actor's process, this is not different from the real Pacino

panhandling on the streets of San Francisco to prep for *Scarecrow* or spending time with Frank Serpico—except, in *Jack and Jill*, Pacino is complicit in portraying this process as utterly absurd.

Once "Pacino" finds a path to playing Quixote he gets into character and doesn't come out— leading to a gag in which Pacino as "Pacino" as Quixote is convinced that a ceiling fan in a bar is a monster and tries to sword-fight it. But in the end, his Method-induced madness is proven to be temporary. The movie closes with Jack showing "Al" the completed Dunkin' Donuts commercial. The ad has Pacino performing a rap and a choreographed hip-hop dance, with famous lines from his movies interwoven with pitches for coffee drinks ("Attica, hoo-ah, latte lite!"), and ends on a freeze-frame of "Pacino" dancing with a human-size coffee cup. Cut to "Pacino" in Jack's office. "Burn this," the actor says. "This must never be seen, by anyone. All copies. Destroy them. Has anyone seen this? They must be found, and talked to." Here "Pacino" suddenly and adamantly rejects this literal regurgitation of his greatest hits, thereby reverting to his persona of a serious actor with integrity. Order is restored for "Al Pacino," but what about the real Al Pacino? After gamely allowing his persona to be subverted for most of the movie, could the actor just press reset and go back, too?

Comparison Between "Al Pacino" in *Jack and Jill* and Pacino's Presentation of Himself in *Looking for Richard*

In *Jack and Jill*, Al Pacino plays "Al Pacino," a famous actor who has an identity crisis while appearing in a stage production of *Richard III*. Call it typecasting: the first time Pacino starred in a feature film "as himself" it was his 1996 directorial debut, *Looking for Richard*, which also featured a glimpse at a contemplative Pacino playing Shakespeare's Machiavellian character. Pacino has called *Richard* a "docudrama," which is accurate in that it's a document of the staging of a drama. "It has always been a dream of mine to communicate how I feel about Shakespeare to other people," he explains via voice-over, declaring his intention to stage a version of the play for the camera, hoping he can "communicate a Shakespeare that's about how we think and feel today." *Jack and Jill*, meanwhile, is a farce that takes place in a heightened world, and so it follows that its characterization of Pacino would include quite a bit of fictionalization. But the mark of caricature is that it's both exaggerated and identifiable, and however self-parodic the character might be, there are elements of the "Al Pacino" in *Jack and Jill* that jibe with the version of himself that the actor/director put forward in *Looking for Richard*. On a basic level, *Richard* is Pacino's attempt to demystify Shakespeare to make it accessible to a modern general audience, while *Jack and Jill* seems to be Pacino's attempt to demystify himself to a modern, general audience, who may have a notion of who he is from his most quotable films, but who are too young to have experienced the peak of his stardom while it was happening. The goal of the Pacino of *Richard* is to serve as a bridge between esoteric art and the common man; by starring as himself in *Jack and Jill*, Pacino becomes that bridge. Both films include aspects of self-consciousness and self-parody, suggesting that Pacino is aware that he has a reputation for being "serious" that doesn't match his conception of himself as a clown. And, in intercutting Pacino's process of finding a character through research and conversation with footage of him performing that character, *Richard* deconstructs how he blurs the lines between off stage and on stage, between character and actor, between real and fiction. The "Pacino" of *Jack and Jill* engages in a similar research process, preparing to play Don Quixote by spending time with Jill, who he considers to be his real-life Dulcinea, learning about how to play madness by submitting to it. And of course, the comedy as a whole is dedicated to blurring the line between the real Al Pacino and the "Pacino" he plays in the movie. The most significant similarity between the Al Pacino of *Looking for Richard* and the "Al Pacino" of *Jack and Jill* may be their common connection to Shakespeare's two-faced king. As a Method actor, drawing on his own past experience is part of Pacino's process, so playing "Al Pacino" playing Richard III allows him to draw on his real experience with the role, as documented in *Richard*. Given that *Richard III* is itself a work of fiction based on real people and events, there perhaps could be no better play to serve as the crux between *Looking for Richard*'s documentary exploration of Pacino's process of character creation and *Jack and Jill*'s playful fictional exploration of "Al Pacino's" process of character creation.

Jack and Jill was one of the most critically reviled movies in years (as of this writing, the film has a 3 percent fresh rating on the review aggregator site Rotten Tomatoes), and Pacino did not emerge unscathed. But while some critics issued backhanded compliments (such as A. O. Scott's assessment, in the *New York Times*, "that this may be Mr. Pacino's most convincing performance in years"[206]), many reviewers who had little good to say about the movie could not help but express awe over Pacino's role in it. Long accused of self-parody, with *Jack and Jill* Pacino made the very notion of "self-parody" literal, and did so with a gusto that few could ignore.

"With bizarre commitment, Pacino endures one indignity after another—as himself, as Richard III and as Don Quixote," wrote the *Hollywood Reporter*. "Why? You start to wonder if they drugged him."[207] In the *New York Times*, Pacino got credit for "giving the film a jolt of genuine zaniness."[208]

"Unlike De Niro, who often sleepwalks through his for-the-paycheck jobs, Pacino gives the movie his all. Method is method, whether you're working with David Mamet or Dennis Dugan," wrote syndicated critic Rene Rodriguez. "His performance is fascinating. This is, arguably, Pacino's first big sellout, but he earns every dollar. He plays himself as an arrogant, show-off manipulator who pitches a fit on stage when someone's cellphone goes off during a performance on Broadway; talks to his service staff in gibberish to make people think he can speak foreign languages; and relentlessly pursues Jill as a way of getting into character for an upcoming role in *Man of La Mancha*... Pacino isn't trying to be funny: He plays everything completely straight, and that's what draws your attention."[209]

Jack and Jill is hard to defend, for a number of reasons. While the exploration of ethnic and class identity through Jack, Jill, and "Pacino" goes surprisingly deep, the subplot involving Jack's Mexican gardener's budding relationship with Jill stumbles into over-the-top, unexamined racial stereotyping. And for all of the narrative's emphasis on authenticity in a world of commercial obligations, the production itself seems to have been substantially subsidized through product placement. The ugly truth is that even as pure entertainment, the movie is really only funny when Pacino is on screen—and sometimes not even then.

But for anyone well acquainted with Pacino's career, the layers of self-reflexivity are fascinating, from the biting direct references (such as the joke about his sole Oscar) to the tossed-off allusions (Jack's palatial home, for instance, has a winding staircase in the foyer reminiscent of Tony's mansion in *Scarface*), to the way the film takes liberties with Pacino's persona and history.

Even as the role requires him to trot out familiar vocal and facial tics (this would have to be the ultimate example of a film on which his main direction was likely, "Give me more Pacino!"), there's also an authentic sense of invention to his performance. He's clearly playing a caricatured version of himself, which often veers into parody not of the real Pacino but of his perception in the collective cultural memory. That the great, serious American actors are often confused with one another is mocked in a scene in which "Al Pacino" begins to tell Jill a story about his past and then pauses and corrects himself: "No, I'm sorry, that was Brando." Pacino explained that he was "play[ing] myself as somebody else," an acting challenge he approached with utmost sincerity. "I tried to keep it real so that the madness is real."[210]

And yet, once the film was on the verge of release, Pacino wondered aloud if the performance didn't represent his own journey into madness. On the red carpet at the *Jack and Jill* premiere, he seemed concerned about the film's reception. "I'm totally crazy," Pacino said. "Maybe I should have winked a little more at the camera." He claimed he wanted to do more comedies, and yet fretted, with arguable seriousness, that the film would ruin his reputation. "If after this picture somebody wants to use me... if they're nuts enough to use me..."[211]

Jack and Jill opened in second place at the US box office, earning $26 million in its first weekend. That number was significantly less than the average opening-weekend haul for an Adam Sandler movie, although the film's final gross of $74 million was the highest for a Pacino movie since *Ocean's Thirteen* in 2007.

It was no surprise that Pacino's tour de force performance as "himself" wasn't exactly heaped with accolades. Instead, Pacino was awarded with the dubious honor of winning a prize at the Golden Raspberry Awards—the cheeky alternative to the Oscars, honoring the year's worst films.

Nominated three times in the past (for *Revolution* in 1985, for *Gigli* in 2003, and for both *88 Minutes* and *Righteous Kill* in 2008), Pacino finally won, for Worst Supporting Actor of 2011. Momentum was on his side, you could say: *Jack and Jill* became the first film in the thirty-two-year history of the Razzies to win in every single category.

For an actor accused of self-parody for so long to go that far in confronting his reputation and attempting to turn it on its head, only to be punished for it? In a sense, this turn of events was foretold by the film itself. *Jack and Jill* is sloppily made and not always consistent in its messages, and yet there's a kernel of valuable truth in its suggestion that while self-knowledge may be essential for an actor, for movie stars self-reflexivity is an unwinnable game.

At the end of *Jack and Jill*, "Al Pacino" sells out.

Please delete address not required before mailing

Affix
stamp
here

PHAIDON PRESS INC.
180 Varick Street
New York
NY 10014

Return address for USA and Canada only

PHAIDON PRESS LIMITED
Regent's Wharf
All Saints Street
London N1 9PA

Return address for UK and countries

Thank you for purchasing a Phaidon book

Sign up to Phaidon Club today at **phaidon.com/club** for special offers, members-only rewards and exclusive invitations to author talks and events. Or just fill out your details below and return this card to the address overleaf that's nearest you to receive our regular email newsletter.

I am interested in the following subjects:

☐ Architecture ☐ Art ☐ Children's ☐ Collector's Editions
☐ Decorative Arts ☐ Design ☐ Fashion ☐ Film
☐ Food ☐ Music ☐ Photography ☐ Travel

I would like to receive information about books in the following languages:

☐ English ☐ French ☐ Italian ☐ Spanish

First Name   Last Name

Town   State/Region   Country

Email address

Your occupation

Which book have you just bought?

Where did you buy this book?

☐ Tick here if you do not wish to receive regular updates on new releases, special offers and exclusive events from Phaidon

Conclusion

A go-for-broke gamble that didn't pay off, *Jack and Jill* joined a roster of twenty-first century Al Pacino films — *Ocean's Thirteen*, *Two for the Money*, *S1m0ne*, *88 Minutes*, *Righteous Kill* — ranging from amusing to forgettable to execrable. Much has changed in the nearly thirty years since the reception of failed experiments like *Scarface* and *Revolution* soured Pacino on Hollywood, and yet once again, during this time of uneven cinematic efforts, Pacino has found fulfillment in the theater. This time around, the stage hasn't been so much an escape from Pacino's screen work as a complement to it. After starring as Shylock in Michael Radford's 2004 film adaptation of *The Merchant of Venice*, Pacino triumphantly reprised the role in Central Park in 2009, and then on Broadway the following year. In August 2012, a new Broadway production of David Mamet's *Glengarry Glen Ross* was announced for the fall season, starring Pacino as Shelley Levene, the part played in the 1992 film version by Jack Lemmon (Bobby Cannavale has been cast as Ricky Roma, the role Pacino played in the movie). He also won Emmy Awards for starring roles based on real people in two HBO TV movies: as Roy Cohn in Mike Nichols's adaptation of the Tony Kushner play *Angels in America* and as "Dr. Death" Jack Kevorkian in Barry Levinson's *You Don't Know Jack*. On deck for 2012 is a third appearance as a notorious real figure in an HBO film: Phil Spector. "Some of the roles that are challenging are more in theater and TV," Pacino acknowledged in 2010. "In movies there's a tendency to cast actors in roles that have been successful for them. It has to pay for itself."[212]

With the compromises required by the ever more corporate culture industry colliding with his advancing age, is it safe to say Al Pacino's best movie work is behind him? It's perhaps not an encouraging sign of forward motion that even as he has been busier than ever (as of this writing, Pacino has five films in some stage of production), the actor has spent the last half decade collecting accolades for past achievements, his rounds on the lifetime-achievement circuit culminating with the National Medal of Arts awarded to Pacino by President Barack Obama at the White House in February 2012.

And yet, his golden oldies resist the mothball treatment; movies Pacino starred in nearly forty years ago continue to inspire and drive the culture. *GQ* magazine recently cast actor/screenwriter Justin Theroux in a photo spread aping *Serpico*; in *James Franco's Cruising*, the polyglot plays the Pacino part in a short film imaginatively re-creating sexually explicit material that William Friedkin was forced to cut from his 1979 gay-nightlife-themed noir. At age seventy-two, Pacino himself cannot seem to slow down. "I always say that I'm going to be selective," Pacino said in 2011 while promoting his most recent production, a theatrical docudrama he starred in and directed in the vein of *Looking for Richard* called *Wilde Salomé*. "But I never am. I always wind up doing something."[213]

Following pages: Al Pacino at the Actors Studio, New York, 2004.

173

1940
April 25: Born Alfredo James Pacino in the Bronx, New York City.

1942
Pacino's parents divorce; the two-year-old moves with his mother to the home of his Sicilian grandparents, Kate and James Gerard.

1957
Pacino drops out of New York's High School of Performing Arts, which angers his mother. He leaves home. Rejected by the Actors Studio, he joins the HB Studio, run by Herbert Berghof and Uta Hagen, where he meets and befriends Charlie Laughton.

1962
Pacino's mother dies. Still estranged from her at the time of her death, the twenty-two-year-old Pacino is deeply regretful.

1966
Successfully auditions for the Actors Studio. Studies under Lee Strasberg, who becomes a close friend. Meets Martin Bregman and becomes his client, forming a partnership that will last for decades, with Bregman finding and/or producing many of Pacino's most successful films.

1967
First paying job as an actor, in a Boston production of *Awake and Sing*.

Meets and starts dating actress Jill Clayburgh.

1968
Makes Off-Broadway debut in *The Indian Wants the Bronx*, opposite John Cazale. Both Cazale and Pacino would win Obie Awards.

1969
Makes Broadway debut in *Does a Tiger Wear a Necktie?*; wins first Tony Award for supporting actor. Makes film debut with one scene in *Me, Natalie*.

1971
Cast in his first leading film role, in Jerry Schatzberg's *The Panic in Needle Park*.

1972
After seeing Pacino in *The Panic in Needle Park*, Francis Ford Coppola fights to cast the relative unknown in the part of Michael Corleone in *The Godfather*. Pacino is nominated for his first Oscar, as Supporting Actor. Five-year relationship with Jill Clayburgh comes to an end. Starts dating Tuesday Weld.

1973
Scarecrow, starring Pacino and Gene Hackman, wins the Palme d'or at the Cannes Film Festival. Plays Richard III for the first time in Boston. Plays real-life NYPD detective Frank Serpico in *Serpico*; is nominated for his first Best Actor Oscar.

1974
Reprises the role of Michael Corleone in *The Godfather Part II*; is nominated for the Best Actor Oscar.

1975
Plays Sonny, a bisexual bank robber based on the real-life John Wojtowicz in *Dog Day Afternoon*. Wins the Los Angeles Film Critics and BAFTA best actor awards for his performance; nominated for his fourth Oscar.

1977
Quits drinking. Stars as a race car driver in *Bobby Deerfield*; begins dating costar Marthe Keller.

1979
Stars as a beleaguered defense attorney in *...And Justice for All*. Nominated for the Oscar yet again.

1980
Stars in William Friedkin's controversial *Cruising*.

1982
Friend and mentor Lee Strasberg dies; Pacino steps in as coartistic director of the Actors Studio.

1983
Stars in Brian De Palma's *Scarface*.

1985
Stars in *Revolution*. Following its failure, Pacino takes a hiatus from film. Finances and stars in short film *The Local Stigmatic*, directed by David Wheeler.

It goes unreleased until a 2007 DVD.

1989
Returns to the big screen in *Sea of Love*. His first film in four years, it's a hit. Acting coach Jan Tarrant gives birth to Pacino's first child, his daughter Julie.

1990
Nominated for an Oscar for his supporting performance as Big Boy Caprice in *Dick Tracy*. Returns to the role of Michael Corleone in *The Godfather Part III*.

1992
Stars in *Scent of a Woman*, and wins his first Oscar, for Best Actor. Is also nominated for his supporting performance in *Glengarry Glen Ross*, making him the first actor to receive two nominations in the same year and win for Best Actor.

1993
Stars in *Carlito's Way* opposite Sean Penn.

1995
Stars opposite Robert De Niro in Michael Mann's *Heat*.

1996
Produces, directs, and appears in *Looking for Richard*, a nonfiction exploration of Shakespeare's *Richard III*. Begins dating actress Beverly D'Angelo. Costars as a satanic lawyer in *Devil's Advocate*.

1999
Appears in *The Insider* and *Any Given Sunday.*

2000
Beverly D'Angelo gives birth to Pacino's twins, Anton and Olivia.

2001
Awarded the Cecil B. DeMille lifetime achievement award at the Golden Globes.

2003
Pacino and D'Angelo split. Stars as the AIDS-afflicted lawyer Roy Cohn in the HBO miniseries of Mike Nichols's *Angels in America.*

2004
Stars as Shylock in a film adaptation of *The Merchant of Venice*, directed by Michael Radford.

2005
Moves from New York to Los Angeles to be closer to his twins.

2006
Mounts theatrical production of Oscar Wilde's *Salomé* in Los Angeles.

2007
Gives a rare comedic performance in *Ocean's Thirteen.*
The AFI honors Pacino with their Life Achievement Award.

2010
Makes high-profile return to Broadway, playing Shylock in *The Merchant of Venice.*

2011
Pacino's third feature as director, *Wilde Salomé*, premieres at the Venice Film Festival.
Pacino costars as "Al Pacino" in *Jack and Jill.*

2012
Wins his first Golden Raspberry Award, for Worst Supporting Actor, for *Jack and Jill.*

Page 176:
Top left: Al Pacino at the end of the 1960s.

Top right: Director Sydney Pollack and Al Pacino on the set of *Bobby Deerfield* (1977).

Bottom left: Al Pacino in William Friedkin's *Cruising* (1980).

Bottom right: Al Pacino in Hugh Hudson's *Revolution* (1985).

Opposite:
Top left: Al Pacino in James Foley's *Glengarry Glen Ross* (1992).

Top right: Al Pacino in Christopher Nolan's *Insomnia* (2002).

Bottom left: Al Pacino in Andrew Niccol's *S1m0ne* (2002).

Bottom right: Al Pacino in Michael Radford's *The Merchant of Venice* (2004).

Page 180:
Top left: Arthur Hiller's *Author! Author!* (1982).

Top right: Michael Mann's *Heat* (1995).

Bottom left: Mike Newell's *Donnie Brasco* (1997).

Bottom right: Al Pacino's *Wilde Salomé* (2011).

Page 185: Jon Avnet's *88 Minutes* (2007).

They share the laughter,
the love, the frustration...
and the bathroom.

Anyone can be a father.
But not every father deserves
a standing ovation.

Al Pacino
Author! Author!

TWENTIETH CENTURY-FOX PRESENTS
AN IRWIN WINKLER PRODUCTION
AN ARTHUR HILLER FILM
AL PACINO
"AUTHOR! AUTHOR!"
DYAN CANNON · TUESDAY WELD

H E A T

AN EPIC SAGA OF CRIME AND OBSESSION

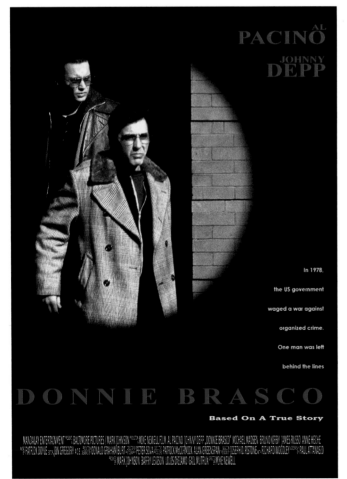

AL
PACINO

JOHNNY
DEPP

In 1978,

the US government

waged a war against

organized crime.

One man was left

behind the lines

D O N N I E   B R A S C O

Based On A True Story

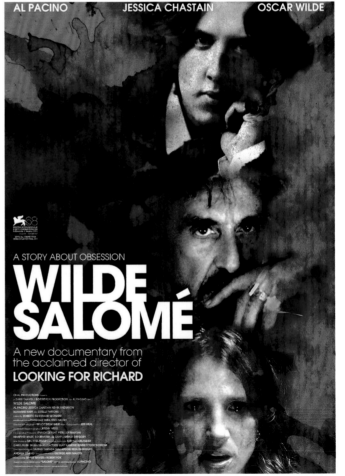

AL PACINO   JESSICA CHASTAIN   OSCAR WILDE

A STORY ABOUT OBSESSION

WILDE SALOMÉ

A new documentary from
the acclaimed director of
LOOKING FOR RICHARD

1969
Me, Natalie
Directed by Fred Coe *Screenplay* A. Martin Zweiback, based on a story by Stanley Shapiro and A. Martin Zweiback *Cinematography* Arthur J. Ornitz *Original Music* Henry Mancini *Film Editing* Sheila Bakerman and John McSweeney Jr. *Produced by* Stanley Shapiro. With Al Pacino (Tony), Patty Duke (Natalie Miller), James Farentino (David Harris), Martin Balsam (Uncle Harold), Elsa Lanchester (Miss Dennison), Salome Jens (Shirley Norton), Nancy Marchand (Mrs. Miller).

1971
The Panic in Needle Park
Directed by Jerry Schatzberg *Screenplay* Joan Didion and John Gregory Dunne, based on a novel by James Mills *Cinematography* Adam Holender *Set Decoration* Philip Smith *Film Editing* Evan A. Lottman *Produced by* Dominick Dunne. With Al Pacino (Bobby), Kitty Winn (Helen), Alan Vint (Detective Hotch), Richard Bright (Hank), Kiel Martin (Chico), Michael McClanathan (Sonny), Warren Finnerty (Sammy).

1972
The Godfather
Directed by Francis Ford Coppola *Screenplay* Francis Ford Coppola and Mario Puzo, based on his novel *Cinematography* Gordon Willis *Set Decoration* Philip Smith *Original Music* Nino Rota *Film Editing* William Reynolds and Peter Zinner *Produced by* Albert S. Ruddy, Gray Frederickson, and Robert Evans. With Al Pacino (Michael Corleone), Marlon Brando (Don Vito Corleone), John Cazale (Fredo Corleone), James Caan (Santino "Sonny" Corleone), Robert Duvall (Tom Hagen), Diane Keaton (Kay Adams), Talia Shire (Connie Corleone Rizzi), Richard Conte (Emilio Barzini).

1973
Scarecrow
Directed by Jerry Schatzberg *Screenplay* Garry Michael White *Cinematography* Vilmos Zsigmond *Original Music* Fred Myrow *Film Editing* Evan A. Lottman *Produced by* Robert M. Sherman. With Al Pacino (Francis Lionel "Lion" Delbuchi), Gene Hackman (Max Millan), Dorothy Tristan (Coley), Ann Wedgeworth (Frenchy), Penelope Allen (Annie Gleason).

Serpico
Directed by Sidney Lumet *Screenplay* Waldo Salt and Norman Wexler, based on a novel by Peter Maas *Cinematography* Arthur J. Ornitz *Set Decoration* Thomas H. Wright *Original Music* Mikis Theodorakis *Film Editing* Dede Allen *Produced by* Martin Bregman, Dino De Laurentiis, and Roger M. Rothstein. With Al Pacino (Frank Serpico), John Randolph (Sidney Green), Jack Kehoe (Tom Keough), Biff McGuire (Captain McClain), Barbara Eda-Young (Laurie), Cornelia Sharpe (Leslie), Tony Roberts (Bob Blair).

1974
The Godfather Part II
Directed by Francis Ford Coppola *Screenplay* Francis Ford Coppola and Mario Puzo, based on his novel *Cinematography* Gordon Willis *Set Decoration* George R. Nelson *Original Music* Nino Rota *Film Editing* Barry Malkin, Richard Marks, and Peter Zinner *Produced by* Francis Ford Coppola, Gray Frederickson, and Fred Roos. With Al Pacino (Michael Corleone), Robert Duvall (Tom Hagen), Diane Keaton (Kay Adams), Robert De Niro (Don Vito Corleone), John Cazale (Fredo Corleone), Talia Shire (Connie Corleone Rizzi), Lee Strasberg (Hyman Roth).

1975
Dog Day Afternoon
Directed by Sidney Lumet *Screenplay* Frank Pierson, based on an article by P. F. Kluge and Thomas Moore *Cinematography* Victor J. Kemper *Set Decoration* Robert Drumheller *Film Editing* Dede Allen *Produced by* Martin Bregman and Martin Elfand. With Al Pacino (Sonny Wortzik), Penelope Allen (Sylvia), Sully Boyar (Mulvaney), John Cazale (Sal), Beulah Garrick (Margaret), James Broderick (Sheldon), Charles Durning (Detective Eugene Moretti), Chris Sarandon (Leon Shermer).

1977
Bobby Deerfield
Directed by Sydney Pollack *Screenplay* Alvin Sargent, based on a novel by Erich Maria Remarque *Cinematography* Henri Decaë *Set Decoration* Gabriel Béchir *Original Music* Dave Grusin *Film Editing* Fredric Steinkamp *Produced by* Sydney Pollack and John Foreman. With Al Pacino (Bobby Deerfield), Marthe Keller (Lillian Morelli), Anny Duperey (Lydia), Romolo Valli (Uncle Luigi), Stephan Meldegg (Karl Holtzman).

1979
...And Justice for All
Directed by Norman Jewison *Screenplay* Valerie Curtin and Barry Levinson *Cinematography* Victor J. Kemper *Set Decoration* Thomas L. Roysden *Original Music* Dave Grusin *Film Editing* John F. Burnett *Produced by* Norman Jewison and Patrick J. Palmer. With Al Pacino (Arthur Kirkland), Jack Warden (Judge Francis Rayford), John Forsythe (Judge Henry T. Fleming), Lee Strasberg (Grandpa Sam), Jeffrey Tambor (Jay Porter), Christine Lahti (Gail Packer).

1980
Cruising
Directed by William Friedkin *Screenplay* William Friedkin, based on a novel by Gerald Walker *Cinematography* James A. Contner *Set Decoration* Robert Drumheller *Original Music* Jack Nitzche *Film Editing* Bud S. Smith *Produced by*

Jerry Weintraub. With Al Pacino (Steve Burns), Paul Sorvino (Captain Edelson), Karen Allen (Nancy), Richard Cox (Stuart Richards), Don Scardino (Ted Bailey).

1982
Author! Author!
Directed by Arthur Hiller *Screenplay* Israel Horovitz *Cinematography* Victor J. Kemper *Set Decoration* Alan Hicks and Harold McConnell Jr. *Original Music* Dave Grusin *Film Editing* William Reynolds *Produced by* Irwin Winkler. With Al Pacino (Ivan Travalian), Dyan Cannon (Alice Detroit), Tuesday Weld (Gloria Travalian), Bob Dishy (Morris Finestein), Bob Elliott (Patrick Dickler).

1983
Scarface
Directed by Brian De Palma *Screenplay* Oliver Stone, based on a novel by Armitage Trail *Cinematography* John A. Alonzo *Set Decoration* Bruce Weintraub *Original Music* Giorgio Moroder *Film Editing* Jerry Greenberg and David Ray *Produced by* Martin Bregman. With Al Pacino (Tony Montana), Steven Bauer (Manny Ribera), Michelle Pfeiffer (Elvira Hancock), Mary Elizabeth Mastrantonio (Gina Montana), Robert Loggia (Frank Lopez).

1985
Revolution
Directed by Hugh Hudson *Screenplay* Robert Dillon *Cinematography* Bernard Lutic *Set Decoration* Ann Mollo *Original Music* John Corigliano *Film Editing* Stuart Baird *Produced by* Irwin Winkler. With Al Pacino (Tom Dobb), Donald Sutherland (Sergent Major Peasy), Nastassja Kinski (Daisy McConnahay), Joan Plowright (Mrs. McConnahay), Dave King (Mr. McConnahay).

1989
Sea of Love
Directed by Harold Becker *Screenplay* Richard Price *Cinematography* Ronnie Taylor *Set Decoration* Gordon Sim *Original Music* Trevor Jones *Film Editing* David Bretherton *Produced by* Martin Bregman and Louis A. Stroller. With Al Pacino (Detective Frank Keller), Ellen Barkin (Helen Cruger), John Goodman (Detective Sherman Touhey), Michael Rooker (Terry), William Hickey (Frank Keller Sr.), Richard Jenkins (Gruber).

1990
The Local Stigmatic
Directed by David F. Wheeler and Al Pacino *Screenplay* Heathcote Williams, based on his play *Cinematography* Ed Lachman *Original Music* Howard Shore *Film Editing* Norman Hollyn *Produced by* Michael Hadge and Al Pacino. With Al Pacino (Graham), Paul Guilfoyle (Ray), Joseph Maher (David).

Dick Tracy
Directed by Warren Beatty *Screenplay* Jim Cash and Jack Epps Jr., based on characters created by Chester Gould *Cinematography* Vittorio Storaro *Set Decoration* Rick Simpson *Original Music* Danny Elfman *Film Editing* Richard Marks *Produced by* Warren Beatty. With Al Pacino (Big Boy Caprice), Warren Beatty (Dick Tracy), Charlie Korsmo (Kid), Michael Donovan O'Donnell (McGillicuddy), Jim Wilkey (Stooge), Stig Eldred (Shoulders).

The Godfather Part III
Directed by Francis Ford Coppola *Screenplay* Mario Puzo and Francis Ford Coppola *Cinematography* Gordon Willis *Set Decoration* Dean Tavoularis *Original Music* Carmine Coppola *Film Editing* Lisa Fruchtman, Barry Malkin, and Walter

Murch *Produced by* Francis Ford Coppola, Gray Frederickson, Charles Mulvehill, and Fred Roos. With Al Pacino (Michael Corleone), Diane Keaton (Kay Adams Michelson), Talia Shire (Connie Corleone Rizzi), Andy Garcia (Vincent Mancini), Eli Wallach (Don Altobello).

1991
Frankie and Johnny
Directed by Garry Marshall *Screenplay* Terrence McNally, based on his play *Cinematography* Dante Spinotti *Set Decoration* Kathe Klopp *Original Music* Marvin Hamlisch *Film Editing* Jacqueline Cambas and Battle Davis *Produced by* Garry Marshall and Nick Abdo. With Al Pacino (Johnny), Michelle Pfeiffer (Frankie), Hector Elizondo (Nick), Nathan Lane (Tim), Kate Nelligan (Cora).

1992
Glengarry Glen Ross
Directed by James Foley *Screenplay* David Mamet, based on his play *Cinematography* Juan Ruiz Anchía *Set Decoration* Robert J. Franco *Original Music* James Newton Howard *Film Editing* Howard E. Smith *Produced by* Jerry Tokofsky, Stanley R. Zupnik, Morris Ruskin, and Joseph M. Caracciolo Jr. With Al Pacino (Ricky Roma), Jack Lemmon (Shelley Levene), Alec Baldwin (Blake), Alan Arkin (George Aaronow), Ed Harris (Dave Moss), Kevin Spacey (John Williamson).

Scent of a Woman
Directed by Martin Brest *Screenplay* Bo Goldman, based on a novel by Giovanni Arpino and on a screenplay by Ruggero Maccari and Dino Risi for *Scent of a Woman* (1974) *Cinematography* Donald E. Thorin *Set Decoration* George DeTitta Jr.

Original Music Thomas Newman *Film Editing* William Steinkamp, Michael Tronick, and Harvey Rosenstock *Produced by* Martin Brest, G. Mac Brown, and Ronald L. Schwary. With Al Pacino (Lieutenant Colonel Frank Slade), Chris O'Donnell (Charlie Simms), James Rebhorn (Mr. Trask), Philip Seymour Hoffman (George Willis Jr.), Gabrielle Anwar (Donna).

1993
Carlito's Way
Directed by Brian De Palma *Screenplay* David Koepp, based on novels by Edwin Torres *Cinematography* Stephen H. Burum *Set Decoration* Leslie A. Pope *Original Music* Patrick Doyle *Film Editing* Kristina Boden and Bill Pankow *Produced by* Martin Bregman, Michael Bregman, and Willi Baer. With Al Pacino (Carlito "Charlie" Brigante), Sean Penn (David Kleinfeld), Penelope Ann Miller (Gail), John Leguizamo (Benny Blanco), Ingrid Rogers (Steffie).

1995
Two Bits
Directed by James Foley *Screenplay* Joseph Stefano *Cinematography* Juan Ruiz Anchía *Set Decoration* Robert J. Franco *Original Music* Carter Burwell *Film Editing* Howard E. Smith *Produced by* Arthur Cohn. With Al Pacino (Grandpa Gitano Sabatoni), Jerry Barone (Gennaro), Mary Elizabeth Mastrantonio (Luisa Spirito), Patrick Borriello (Tullio), Andy Romano (Dr. Bruna), Donna Mitchell (Mrs. Bruna), Mary Lou Rosato (Aunt Carmela), Joe Grifasi (Uncle Joe).

Heat
Directed by Michael Mann *Screenplay* Michael Mann *Cinematography* Dante Spinotti *Set Decoration* Anne H. Ahrens *Original*

Music Elliot Goldenthal *Film Editing* Pasquale Buba, and Dov Hoenig *Produced by* Art Linson and Michael Mann. With Al Pacino (Lieutenant Vincent Hanna), Robert De Niro (Neil McCauley), Val Kilmer (Chris Shiherlis), Jon Voight (Nate), Tom Sizemore (Michael Cheritto), Diane Venora (Justine Hanna).

1996
City Hall
Directed by Harold Becker *Screenplay* Ken Lipper, Paul Schrader, Nicholas Pileggi, and Bo Goldman *Cinematography* John Corso and Michael Seresin *Set Decoration* Robert J. Franco and Bruce Swanson *Original Music* Jerry Goldsmith *Film Editing* David Bretherton and Robert C. Jones *Produced by* Harold Becker, Ken Lipper, Charles Mulvehill, and Edward R. Pressman. With Al Pacino (Mayor John Pappas), John Cusack (Deputy Mayor Kevin Calhoun), Bridget Fonda (Marybeth Cogan), Danny Aiello (Frank Anselmo), Martin Landau (Judge Walter Stern), David Paymer (Abe Goodman).

Looking for Richard
Directed by Al Pacino *Screenplay* Al Pacino and Frederic Kimball, based on a play by William Shakespeare *Cinematography* Robert Leacock *Original Music* Howard Shore *Film Editing* William A. Anderson, Ned Bastille, Pasquale Buba, and Andre Ross Betz *Produced by* Al Pacino and Michael Hadge. With Al Pacino (Himself/Richard III), Penelope Allen (Herself/Queen Elizabeth), Gordon MacDonald (Himself/Dorset), Madison Arnold (Himself/Rivers), Vincent Angell (Himself/Grey), Harris Yulin (Himself/King Edward), Alec Baldwin (Himself/Duke of Clarence).

1997
Donnie Brasco
Directed by Mike Newell *Screenplay* Paul Attanasio, based on a novel by Joseph D. Pistone and Richard Woodley *Cinematography* Peter Sova *Set Decoration* Leslie A. Pope *Original Music* Patrick Doyle *Film Editing* Jon Gregory *Produced by* Louis DiGiaimo, Mark Johnson, Barry Levinson, and Gail Mutrux. With Al Pacino (Benjamin "Lefty" Ruggiero), Johnny Depp (Donnie Brasco/Joseph D. "Joe" Pistone), Michael Madsen (Sonny Black), Bruno Kirby (Nicky), James Russo (Paulie), Anne Heche (Maggie Pistone), Zeljko Ivanek (Tim Curley).

Devil's Advocate
Directed by Taylor Hackford *Screenplay* Jonathan Lemkin and Tony Gilroy, based on a novel by Andrew Neiderman *Cinematography* Andrzej Bartkowiak *Set Decoration* Roberta J. Holinko *Original Music* James Newton Howard *Film Editing* Mark Warner *Produced by* Anne Kopelson, Arnold Kopelson, and Arnon Milchan. With Al Pacino (John Milton), Keanu Reeves (Kevin Lomax), Charlize Theron (Mary Ann Lomax), Jeffrey Jones (Eddie Barzoon), Judith Ivey (Mrs. Alice Lomax), Connie Nielsen (Christabella Andreoli).

1999
The Insider
Directed by Michael Mann *Screenplay* Eric Roth and Michael Mann, based on an article by Marie Brenner *Cinematography* Dante Spinotti *Original Music* Pieter Bourke and Lisa Gerrard *Film Editing* William Goldenberg, David Rosenbloom, and Paul Rubell *Produced by* Pieter Jan Brugge and Michael Mann. With Al Pacino (Lowell Bergman), Russell Crowe (Jeffrey Wigand), Christopher Plummer (Mike Wallace), Diane Venora (Liane Wigand),

Philip Baker Hall (Don Hewitt), Lindsay Crouse (Sharon Tiller).

Any Given Sunday
Directed by Oliver Stone *Screenplay* John Logan and Oliver Stone, based on a screen story by Daniel Pyne and John Logan *Cinematography* Salvatore Totino *Set Decoration* Ronald R. Reiss and Ford Wheeler *Original Music* Richard Horowitz and Paul Kelly *Film Editing* Stuart Levy, Thomas J. Nordberg, Keith Salmon, and Stuart Waks *Produced by* Dan Halsted, Lauren Shuler Donner, and Clayton Townsend. With Al Pacino (Tony D'Amato), Cameron Diaz (Christina Pagniacci), Dennis Quaid (Jack "Cap" Rooney), James Woods (Dr. Harvey Mandrake), Jamie Foxx (Willie Beamen), LL Cool J (Julian Washington).

2000
Chinese Coffee
Directed by Al Pacino *Screenplay* Ira Lewis, based on her play *Cinematography* Frank Prinzi *Set Decoration* Carol Silverman *Original Music* Elmer Bernstein *Film Editing* Michael Berenbaum, Pasquale Buba, and Noah Herzog *Produced by* Michael Hadge, Larry Meistrich, and Robert Salerno. With Al Pacino (Harry Levine), Jerry Orbach (Jake Manheim), Susan Floyd (Joanna), Ellen McElduff (Mavis), Michel Moinot (Maurice).

2002
People I Know
Directed by Daniel Algrant *Screenplay* Jon Robin Baitz *Cinematography* Peter Deming *Set Decoration* Andrew Baseman *Original Music* Terence Blanchard *Film Editing* Suzy Elmiger *Produced by* Michael Nozik, Karen Tenkhoff, and Leslie Urdang. With Al Pacino

(Eli Wurman), Kim Basinger (Victoria Gray), Ryan O'Neal (Cary Launer), Téa Leoni (Jilli Hopper), Richard Schiff (Elliot Sharansky).

Insomnia
Directed by Christopher Nolan *Screenplay* Hillary Seitz, based on a screenplay by Nikolaj Frobenius, and Erik Skjoldbjærg *Cinematography* Wally Pfister *Set Decoration* Peter Lando *Original Music* David Julyan *Film Editing* Dody Dorn *Produced by* Broderick Johnson, Paul Junger Witt, Andrew A. Kosove, and Edward McDonnell. With Al Pacino (Will Dormer), Robin Williams (Walter Finch), Hilary Swank (Ellie Burr), Oliver "Ole" Zemen (Pilot), Martin Donovan (Hap Eckhart), Paul Dooley (Chief Nyback).

S1m0ne
Directed by Andrew Niccol *Screenplay* Andrew Niccol *Cinematography* Edward Lachman *Set Decoration* Leslie A. Pope *Original Music* Carter Burwell *Film Editing* Paul Rubell *Produced by* Andrew Niccol. With Al Pacino (Viktor Taransky), Benjamin Salisbury (Production Assistant), Winona Ryder (Nicola Anders), Darnell Williams (Studio Executive #1), Jim Rash (Studio Executive #2), Ron Perkins (Studio Executive #3), Jay Mohr (Hal Sinclair), Catherine Keener (Elaine Christian), Evan Rachel Wood (Lainey Christian Taransky).

2003
The Recruit
Directed by Roger Donaldson *Screenplay* Roger Towne, Kurt Wimmer, and Mitch Glazer *Cinematography* Stuart Dryburgh *Set Decoration* Peter P. Nicolakakos *Original Music* Klaus Badelt *Film Editing* David Rosenbloom *Produced by* Jeff Apple, Gary Barber, and Roger Birnbaum.

With Al Pacino (Walter Burke), Colin Farrell (James Douglas Clayton), Bridget Moynahan (Layla Moore), Gabriel Macht (Zack), Kenneth Mitchell (Alan), Mike Realba (Ronnie Gibson).

Gigli
Directed by Martin Brest *Screenplay* Martin Brest *Cinematography* Robert Elswit *Set Decoration* Maggie Martin *Original Music* John Powell *Film Editing* Julie Monroe and Billy Weber *Produced by* Martin Brest and Casey Silver. With Al Pacino (Starkman), Ben Affleck (Larry Gigli), Jennifer Lopez (Ricki), Lenny Venito (Louis), Justin Bartha (Brian), Christopher Walken (Stanley Jacobellis).

Angels in America (TV miniseries)
Directed by Mike Nichols *Screenplay* Tony Kushner *Cinematography* Stephen Goldblatt *Set Decoration* George DeTitta Jr. *Original Music* Thomas Newman *Film Editing* John Bloom and Antonia Van Drimmelen *Produced by* Celia D. Costas. With Al Pacino (Roy Cohn), Justin Kirk (Prior Walter), Ben Shenkman (Louis Ironson), Emma Thompson (Nurse Emily), Patrick Wilson (Joe Pitt), Jeffrey Wright (Belize), Meryl Streep (Ethel Rosenberg).

2004
The Merchant of Venice
Directed by Michael Radford *Screenplay* Michael Radford, based on a play by William Shakespeare *Cinematography* Benoît Delhomme *Set Decoration* Gillie Delap *Original Music* Jocelyn Pook *Film Editing* Lucia Zucchetti *Produced by* Cary Brokaw, Barry Navidi, Jason Piette, and Michael Lionello Cowen. With Al Pacino (Shylock), Jeremy Irons (Antonio), Joseph Fiennes (Bassanio), Lynn Collins (Portia), Zuleikha Robinson (Jessica), Kris Marshall (Gratiano), Charlie Cox (Lorenzo).

2005
Two for the Money
Directed by D. J. Caruso *Screenplay* Dan Gilroy *Cinematography* Conrad W. Hall *Set Decoration* Mary-Lou Storey *Original Music* Christophe Beck *Film Editing* Glen Scantlebury *Produced by* Jay Cohen and James G. Robinson. With Al Pacino (Walter Abrams), Matthew McConaughey (Brandon), Rene Russo (Toni), Armand Assante (Novian), Jeremy Piven (Jerry), Jaime King (Alexandria), Kevin Chapman (Southie).

2007
88 Minutes
Directed by Jon Avnet *Screenplay* Gary Scott Thompson *Cinematography* Denis Lenoir *Set Decoration* Dominique Fauquet-Lemaitre *Original Music* Ed Shearmur *Film Editing* Peter E. Berger *Produced by* Jon Avnet, Randall Emmett and Gary Scott Thompson. With Al Pacino (Jack Gramm), Alicia Witt (Kim Cummings), Leelee Sobieski (Lauren Douglas), Amy Brenneman (Shelly Barnes), William Forsythe (Frank Parks).

Ocean's Thirteen
Directed by Steven Soderbergh *Screenplay* Brian Koppelman and David Levien, based on characters by George Clayton Johnson and Jack Golden Russell *Cinematography* Steven Soderbergh *Set Decoration* Kristen Toscano Messina *Original Music* David Holmes *Film Editing* Stephen Mirrione *Produced by* Jerry Weintraub. With Al Pacino (Willy Bank), George Clooney (Danny Ocean), Brad Pitt (Rusty Ryan), Matt Damon (Linus Caldwell/Lenny Pepperidge), Michael Mantell (Dr. Stan), Elliott Gould (Reuben Tishkoff), Ray Xifo (Reuben's Butler).

2008
Righteous Kill
Directed by Jon Avnet *Screenplay* Russell Gewirtz *Cinematography* Denis Lenoir *Set Decoration* Kathy Lucas *Original Music* Ed Shearmur *Film Editing* Paul Hirsch *Produced by* Jon Avnet, Rob Cowan, Randall Emmett, Lati Grobman, Avi Lerner, Alexandra Milchan, and Daniel M. Rosenberg. With Al Pacino (Rooster), Robert De Niro (Turk), 50 Cent (Spider), Carla Gugino (Karen Corelli), John Leguizamo (Detective Simon Perez), Donnie Wahlberg (Detective Ted Riley).

2010
You Don't Know Jack (TV movie)
Directed by Barry Levinson *Screenplay* Adam Mazer *Cinematography* Eigil Bryld *Set Decoration* Rena DeAngelo *Original Music* Marcelo Zarvos *Film Editing* Aaron Yanes *Produced by* Scott Ferguson. With Al Pacino (Jack Kevorkian), Brenda Vaccaro (Margo Janus), John Goodman (Neal Nicol), Deirdre O'Connell (Linda), Todd Susman (Stan Levy), Adam Lubarsky (Brian Russell).

2011
Jack and Jill
Directed by Dennis Dugan *Screenplay* Steve Koren and Adam Sandler, based on a story by Ben Zook *Cinematography* Dean Cundey *Set Decoration* Ronald R. Reiss *Original Music* Rupert Gregson-Williams *Film Editing* Tom Costain *Produced by* Adam Sandler, Todd Garner, and Jack Giarraputo. With Al Pacino (Himself), Adam Sandler (Jack Sadelstein/Jill Sadelstein), Katie Holmes (Erin Sadelstein), Elodie Tougne (Sofia Sadelstein), Rohan Chand (Gary Sadelstein).

The Son of No One
Directed by Dito Montiel *Screenplay* Dito Montiel *Cinematography* Benoît Delhomme *Set Decoration* Carrie Stewart *Original Music* Jonathan Elias and David Wittman *Film Editing* Jake Pushinsky *Produced by* Dito Montiel, John Thompson, and Holly Wiersma. With Al Pacino (Detective Charles Stanford), Channing Tatum (Jonathan "Milk" White), James Ransone (Officer Thomas Prudenti), Ray Liotta (Captain Marion Mathers), Katie Holmes (Kerry White).

Wilde Salomé
Directed by Al Pacino *Screenplay* Al Pacino, based on a play by Oscar Wilde *Cinematography* Benoît Delhomme, Robert Leacock, Denis Maloney, and Jeremy Weiss *Original Music* Jeff Beal *Film Editing* Pasquale Buba, David Leonard, Stan Salfas, and Roberto Silvi *Produced by* Robert Fox and Barry Navidi. With Al Pacino (Himself/King Herod), Jessica Chastain (Salomé), Kevin Anderson (Himself/John the Baptist), Roxanne Hart (Herodias), Barry Navidi (Himself).

AL
PACINO

JACK GRAMM HAS
EIGHTY-EIGHT MINUTES
TO SOLVE A MURDER.

HIS OWN.

88
MINUTES

MILLENNIUM FILMS PRESENTS A RANDALL EMMETT/GEORGE FURLA PRODUCTION
FOR EQUITY PICTURES MEDIENFONDS GMBH & KG III AND NU IMAGE ENTERTAINMENT GMBH A JON AVNET FILM
AL PACINO '88 MINUTES' ALICIA WITT LEELEE SOBIESKI AMY BRENNEMAN DEBORAH KARA UNGER
BENJAMIN MCKENZIE AND NEAL McDONOUGH CASTING BY RICK PAGANO, C.S.A. EDITED BY PETER BERGER, A.C.E.
MUSIC BY EDWARD SHEARMUR COSTUME DESIGNER MARY McLEOD DIRECTOR OF PHOTOGRAPHY DENIS LENOIR, A.S.C. A.F.C. PRODUCTION DESIGNER TRACEY GALLACHER
LINE PRODUCER SHAWN WILLIAMSON PRODUCERS GERD KOECHLIN MANFRED HEID JOCHEN KAMLAH MICHAEL FLANNIGAN
EXECUTIVE PRODUCERS AVI LERNER DANNY DIMBORT TREVOR SHORT JOHN THOMPSON GEORGE FURLA BOAZ DAVIDSON

185

Bibliography

Articles

Harvey Aronson, "Al Pacino: *The Godfather* Out of Nowhere!," *Cosmopolitan*, March 1973.

Peter Bart, "The Mob, the Movies and Me," *GQ*, June 1997.

Mel Gussow, "The Basic Training of Al Pacino," *The New York Times*, June 5, 1977.

Paul Haspel, "Arthur on a Quest in Baltimore: Mythic Archetypes, Social Criticism, and Civic Self-Promotion in *...And Justice for All*," *Journal of Popular Film and Television*, Fall 2007.

Gregg Kilday, "Al Pacino on the Lam from *Godfather* Fame," *Los Angeles Times*, June 25, 1972.

Stephen Rebello, "The Resurrection of Tony Montana," *Playboy*, December 2011.

Clarke Taylor, "Lawyer Pacino Carries a Brief for Comedy," *Los Angeles Times*, January 14, 1979.

Bernard Weinraub, "A Foul Mouth with a Following: 20 Years Later, Pacino's 'Scarface' Resonates With a Young Audience," *The New York Times*, September 23, 2003.

Books

Robert Evans, *The Kid Stays in the Picture*, Hyperion, New York, 1994.

Lawrence Grobel, *Al Pacino*, Simon Spotlight Entertainment, New York, 2006.

Nick James, *Heat*, British Film Institute, London, 2002.

Pauline Kael, *For Keeps*, Dutton, New York, 1994.

Harlan Lebo, *The Godfather Legacy*, Fireside/ Simon & Schuster, New York, 1997.

Ken Tucker, *Scarface Nation: The Ultimate Gangster Movie and How It Changed America*, St. Martin's Griffin, New York, 2008.

Andrew Yule, *Al Pacino: A Life on the Wire*, S.P.I. Books, New York, 1992.

Other

Lawrence Grobel, *Reflections on Scarface*. Booklet packaged with *Scarface* Blu-ray DVD in 2011. Accessed at LawrenceGrobel.com.

1 Lawrence Grobel, *Al Pacino in his own words: conversations, 1979–2005*, Simon Spotlight Entertainment, 2006, p. 2.

2 Lawrence Grobel, *op. cit.*, p. 33.

3 Sam Kashner, "Here's to You, Mr. Nichols: The Making of *The Graduate*," *Vanity Fair*, March 2008.

4 *Ibid.*

5 Leonard Maltin, "Two Screen Legends in One Place," *USA Weekend*, September 5, 2008.

6 Brian Rafferty, "When Pacino Was Cool", *GQ*, February 2004.

7 Lawrence Grobel, *op. cit.*, p. 7.

8 Lawrence Grobel, *op. cit.*, pp. 3–4.

9 Rebecca Winters Keegan, "10 Questions for Al Pacino," TIME.com, June 14, 2007.

10 Lawrence Grobel, *op. cit.*, p. 6.

11 Lawrence Grobel, *op. cit.*, p. 6.

12 Guy Flatley, "Al Pacino's Remembrance of Things (and Flings) Past," *Los Angeles Times*, 1973. Accessed at http://www.moviecrazed.com/outpast/alpacdowney.html.

13 Lawrence Grobel, *op. cit.*, p. 7.

14 Andrew Yule, *Al Pacino: A Life on the Wire*, S.P.I. Books, 1992, p. 9.

15 Lawrence Grobel, *op. cit.*, p. 14.

16 Guy Flatley, *op. cit.*

17 Andrew Yule, *op. cit.*, p. 15.

18 "Al Pacino (Season 12, Episode 20)," *Inside the Actors Studio*, October 2, 2006. Television.

19 Bridget Byrene, "Movie Making by Instinct," *Los Angeles Herald-Examiner*, December 17, 1973.

20 Lawrence Grobel, *op. cit.*, p. 79.

21 Andrew Yule, *op. cit.*, p. 42.

22 Lawrence Grobel, *op. cit.*, p. 75.

23 *Jack and Jill* press notes, Universal Pictures, 2011.

24 Jeff Giles, "...And Justice For Al," The Daily Beast, *Newsweek*, June 3, 2002.

25 Harlan Lebo, *The Godfather Legacy*, Simon & Schuster, 1997, p. 63.

26 William Murray, "Playboy Interview: Francis Ford Coppola," *Playboy*, July 1975.

27 Lawrence Grobel, *op. cit.*, p. 23.

28 Robert Evans, *The Kid Stays in the Picture*, Hyperion, 1994, *op. cit.*, p. 221.

29 Lawrence Grobel, *op. cit.*, p. 25.

30 Harvey Aronson, "Al Pacino: The Godfather Out of Nowhere!," *Cosmopolitan*, March 1973.

31 Harlan Lebo, *op. cit.*, p. 108.

32 Lawrence Grobel, *op. cit.*, xxi.

33 Pauline Kael, "*The Godfather*: Alchemy," collected in *For Keeps*, Dutton, 1994, p. 437.

34 Lawrence Grobel, *op. cit.*, p. 27.

35 Lawrence Grobel, *op. cit.*, p. 110.

36 Lawrence Grobel, *op. cit.*, p. 21.

37 Andrew Yule, *op. cit.*, p. 95.

38 William Murray, *op. cit.*

39 *Ibid.*

40 Lawrence Grobel, *op. cit.*, p. 29.

41 *The Godfather Part II* press notes.

42 *The Godfather Part III* DVD commentary, as quoted in Gene D. Phillips's *Godfather: The Intimate Francis Ford Coppola*, The University Press of Kentucky, 2004, p. 130.

43 Lawrence Grobel, *op. cit.*, p. 111.

44 Gene D. Phillips, *op. cit.*, p. 140.

45 Andrew Yule, *op. cit.*, p. 285.

46 Maureen Dowd, "Al Alone," *GQ*, September 1992.

47 *Ibid.*

48 Lawrence Grobel, *op. cit.*, p. 107.

49 Andrew Yule, *op. cit.*, p. 288.

50 Peter Bart, "The Mob, the Movies and Me," *GQ*, June 1997.

51 Gregg Kilday, "Al Pacino on the Lam from *Godfather* Fame," *Los Angeles Times*, June 25, 1972.

52 *Ibid.*

53 "Stars Panhandle on City Streets," *Warner Bros. Rambling Reporter*, January 1973.

54 Mike Snider, "'Scarecrow': Hackman at His Best," *USA Today*, July 11, 2005.

55 Andrew Yule, *op. cit.*, p. 67.

56 Andrew Yule, *op. cit.*, pp. 67–68.

57 Garry Michael White, *Scarecrow*, script, 1973. Unpublished, accessed in AMPAS archives.

58 Christopher Bell, "Jerry Schatzberg's 'Scarecrow' First Had Bill Cosby & Jack Lemmon Attached And 4 Other Things...," Indiewire.com, February 27, 2011.

59 Joy Gould Boyum, "On Film: Scarecrow," *The Wall Street Journal*, April 30, 1973.

60 Murf, "Scarecrow," *Variety*, April 11, 1973.

61 Alan R. Howard, "Movie Review: Scarecrow," *The Hollywood Reporter*, April 9, 1973.

62 Stanley Kauffmann, "Scarecrow," *The New Republic*, May 5, 1973.

63 Lawrence Grobel, *op. cit.*, p. 75.

64 Dave Kehr, "New DVD's," Review of *Scarecrow*, *The New York Times*, July 12, 2005.

65 The phrase "the personal is political" is credited to Carol Hanisch, a radical feminist who published a paper with that title in 1969.

66 Pauline Kael, "The Hero as Freak," collected in

Reeling, Atlantic-Little, Brown, 1976.

67 Sidney Lumet, *Making Movies*, Alfred A. Knopf, 1995, p. 70.

68 Andrew Yule, *op. cit.*, p. 81.

69 Andrew Yule, *op. cit.*, p. 69.

70 *Ibid.*

71 Lawrence Grobel, *op. cit.*, p. 32.

72 *Ibid.*

73 Jeff Giles, *op. cit.*

74 Ironically, Pacino had chosen to do *Serpico* over another film he had been offered at the same time, Bob Fosse's *Lenny*—whose titular lead role, of course, went to Hoffman.

75 Frank Rich, "A Good Cop is Hard to Find," *New Times*, December 12, 1973.

76 Judith Crist, "A Probing of Probity," *New York*, December 10, 1973.

77 Andrew Yule, *op. cit.*, p. 129.

78 Andrew Yule, *op. cit.*, p. 87.

79 Mark Sufrin, "*The Godfather* Al Pacino Superstar of 1975," *SAGA Magazine*, date unknown.

80 Lawrence Grobel, *op. cit.*, p. 45.

81 Lawrence Grobel, *op. cit.*, p. 39.

82 Lawrence Grobel, *op. cit.*, p. 57.

83 Andrew Yule, *op. cit.*, p. 99.

84 Andrew Yule, *op. cit.*, p. 85.

85 Paul Rosenfield, "Actor, Actor", *The Los Angeles Times*, December 29, 1985.

86 Lawrence Grobel, *op. cit.*, p. 180.

87 Arthur Bell, "Littlejohn & the Mob: Saga of a Heist," *The Village Voice*, August 31, 1972.

88 Accessed at http://www.ejumpcut.org/archive/onlinessays/JC15folder/RealDogDay.html.

89 Judson Klinger, "Save Our Script," *American Film*, June 1990.

90 Lawrence Grobel, *op. cit.*, p. 31.

91 "Steve Warren on *Dog Day Afternoon*," *The Advocate*, November 19, 1975.

92 Lawrence Grobel, *op. cit.*, p. 31.

93 Lawrence Grobel, *op. cit.*, p. 133.

94 Sidney Lumet, *op. cit.*, p. 33.

95 Lawrence Grobel, *op. cit.*, p. 141.

96 Lawrence Grobel, *op. cit.*, p. 37.

97 ...*And Justice for All* production notes, Columbia Pictures, 1979.

98 *Ibid.*

99 *Ibid.*

100 *Ibid.*

101 Lawrence Grobel, *op. cit.*, p. 37.

102 Lawrence Grobel, *op. cit.*, p. 39.

103 ...*And Justice for All* production notes.

104 *Ibid.*

105 Clarke Taylor, "Lawyer Pacino Carries a Brief for Comedy," *Los Angeles Times*, January 14, 1979.

106 Norman Jewison, *This Terrible Business Has Been Good to Me*, St. Martin's Press, 2004, p. 206.

107 Lawrence Grobel, *op. cit.*, p. 38.

108 *Ibid.*

109 David Denby, "Abbott and Costello Meet Felix Frankfurter," *New York*, October 29, 1979.

110 Renata Adler, "The Current Cinema: Exasperation," *The New Yorker*, October 22, 1979.

111 Andrew Sarris, "Contempt of Court," *The Village Voice*, October 22, 1979.

112 Charles Champlin, "Justice Approaches the Bench—Skeptically," *Los Angeles Times*, October 14, 1979.

113 Andrew Yule, *op. cit.*, p. 190.

114 Rob Markman, "Al Pacino Thanks Rappers For 'Scarface' Revival," MTV.com. August 25, 2011.

115 Gene Siskel, "'Justice' Perpetrates a Travesty," *Chicago Tribune*, October 19, 1979.

116 Lawrence Grobel, *op. cit.*, p. 84.

117 Lawrence Grobel, *op. cit.*, p. 17.

118 Andrew Yule, *op. cit.*, p. 148.

119 Paul Rosenfield, *op. cit.*

120 Lawrence Grobel, *op. cit.*, p. 46.

121 Lawrence Grobel, "Reflections on *Scarface*," LawrenceGrobel.com.

122 Lawrence Grobel, *op. cit.*, p. 86.

123 Andrew Yule, *op. cit.*, p. 207.

124 Andrew Yule, *op. cit.*, pp. 210–211.

125 Lawrence Grobel, *op. cit.*, p. 132.

126 Andrew Yule, *op. cit.*, p. 227.

127 Simon Hattenstone, "Pacino's Way," *The Guardian*, December 3, 2004.

128 Lawrence Grobel, *op. cit.*, p. 84.

129 Bernard Weinraub, "A Foul Mouth with a Following; 20 Years Later, Pacino's 'Scarface' Resonates with a Young Audience," *The New York Times*, September 23, 2003.

130 Lawrence Grobel, *op. cit.*, p. 86.

131 Lawrence Grobel, *op. cit.*, p. 87.

132 Lawrence Grobel, "Reflections on *Scarface*," *op. cit.*

133 Stephen Rebello, "The Resurrection of Tony Montana," *Playboy*, December 2011.

134 *Ibid.*

135 *Ibid.*

136 Eric Estrin, "Al Pacino is Scarface," *The Movie Magazine*, date unknown.

137 Andrew Yule, *op. cit.*, p. 214.

138 Stephen Rebello, *op. cit.*

139 Lawrence Grobel, *op. cit.*, p. 85.

140 Simon Hattenstone, *op. cit.*

141 Stephen Rebello, *op. cit.*

142 Andrew Yule, *op. cit.*, p. 106.

143 Simon Hattenstone, *op. cit.*

144 Pauline Kael, "A De Palma Movie for People Who Don't Like De Palma Movies," collected in *State of the Art*, Dutton, 1985.

145 Andrew Yule, *op. cit.*, p. 225.

146 Richard Corliss, "Cinema: Say Good Night to the Bad Guy," *TIME*, December 5, 1983.

147 Lawrence Grobel, *op. cit.*, p. 132.

148 Bernard Weinraub, *op. cit.*

149 Stephen Rebello, *op. cit.*

150 Stephen Rebello, *op. cit.*

151 Teresa Carpenter, "Al Pacino: Regular Guy Among Ordinary Joes," *The New York Times*, October 6, 1991.

152 Paul Rosenfield, *op. cit.*

153 Dave Calhoun, "A Bronx Tale," *Time Out London*, November 24, 2004.

154 Lawrence Grobel, *op. cit.*, xxv.

155 F. X. Feeney interview with Richard Price, republished at http://velvet_peach.tripod.com/fpacseaoflove.html.

156 Lawrence Grobel, *op. cit.*, p. 141.

157 Andrew Yule, *op. cit.*, p. 262.

158 Glenn Collins, "A Movie by New Yorkers About New Yorkers," *The New York Times*, September 21, 1988.

159 David Denby, "Looking for Mrs. Goodbar,"

New York, September 18, 1989.

160 Andrew Yule, *op. cit.*, p. 276.

161 David Ansen, "A Detective Falls for a Femme Fatale: Pacino Returns to Form", *Newsweek*, September 18, 1989.

162 Andrew Yule, *op. cit.*, p. 279.

163 Andrew Yule, *op. cit.*, p. 275.

164 Tom Carson, "Phoning It In," *GQ*, April 2004.

165 The monologue that explains the title *Scent of a Woman*. The film is a Hollywood remake of Dino Risi's *Profumo di donna* (1974) with Vittorio Gassman.

166 Steve Grant, "Al Said and Done," *Time Out London*, February 24, 1993.

167 Lawrence Grobel, *op. cit.*, p. 142.

168 Larry Carroll, "Al Pacino Unplugged: Actor on 'Godfather,' 'Heat' and Origin of 'Hoo-Ah!'," MTV.com. See also *Heat* DVD commentary and original screenplay for *Heat*.

169 Peter Rainer, "Pacino Catches the Scent," *Los Angeles Times*, December 23, 1992.

170 David Denby, "One From the Heart," *New York*, December 14, 1992.

171 Terrence Rafferty, "The Enemy Within," *The New Yorker*, December 28, 1992.

172 David J. Fox, "Mopping Up After the Oscars," *Los Angeles Times*, April 4, 1993.

173 Steve Grant, *op. cit.*

174 Jeffrey Wells, "Length of a Woman," *Los Angeles Times*, January 3, 1993.

175 Army Archerd, "Just for Variety," *Variety*, November 12, 1992.

176 Lawrence Grobel, *op. cit.*, p. 128.

177 Roger Ebert, "Heat," *Chicago Sun-Times*, December 15, 1995.

178 Mann quoted in United Artists press notes for *Thief*, quoted in Nick James's *Heat*, London, British Film Institute, 2002, p. 19.

179 Nick James, *op. cit.*, p. 26.

180 Geoff Andrew, "Mann to Man," *Time Out London*, January 17, 1996.

181 Ed Halliwell, "The Method Men," *Empire*, June 2003.

182 *Ibid.*

183 Bernard Weinraub, "De Niro and Pacino Star in a Film. Together," *The New York Times*, July 27, 1985.

184 John Powers, "Pacino's Edgy Genius," *Vogue*, January 1996.

185 Dave Calhoun, "A Bronx Tale," *Time Out London*, November 24, 2004.

186 Will Harris, "Random Roles: Hank Azaria," *AV Club*, September 14, 2011.

187 Larry Carroll, *op. cit.* See also *Heat* DVD commentary and original screenplay for *Heat*.

188 *Ibid.*

189 Cindy Pearlman, "Scent of a Legend," *Chicago Tribune*, December 10, 1995.

190 Geoff Andrew.

191 Ed Halliwell, *op. cit.*

192 Steven Rybin, *The Cinema of Michael Mann*, Lexington, 2007, pp. 190–194.

193 Cindy Pearlman, *op. cit.*

194 Joe Morgenstern, "Heat," *The Wall Street Journal*, December 22, 1995.

195 Rex Reed, *Esquire*, February 2006.

196 Dyland Jones, "De Niro and Pacino: Godfathers of American movies," *Press-Telegram*, January 31, 1996.

197 David Edelstein, "An Offer You Can't Refuse," *New York*, February 21–28, 2011.

198 Stephen Holden, "Feb. 20–26: The Week Ahead," *The New York Times*, February 20, 2011.

199 Drew McWeeny, "Review: Adam Sandler's 'Jack and Jill' One of His Career Worsts," HitFix.com, November 10, 2011.

200 Mark Sufrin, *op. cit.*

201 Simon Hattenstone, *op. cit.*

202 David S. Cohen, "AFI Honoree Arrives with Desire Intact," *Variety*, June 7, 2007.

203 Jesse McKinley and Nichole M. Christian, "Hark, Hark, That Tweet Is No Lark. It's Illegal," *The New York Times*, February 13, 2003.

204 *Jack and Jill* press notes, Universal Pictures, 2011.

205 *Op. cit.*

206 A. O. Scott, "Going Over the Top, Then Downhill," *The New York Times*, November 11, 2011.

207 David Rooney, "Jack and Jill: Film Review," *The Hollywood Reporter*, November 10, 2011.

208 A. O. Scott, *op. cit.*

209 Rene Rodriguez, "Sandler's *Jack and Jill* Is a Real Drag," *McClatchy Newspapers*, November 11, 2011.

210 *Jack and Jill* press notes.

211 Lauren Zima, "Adam Sandler Gets Ribbed," *Variety*, November 8, 2011.

212 Jason Zinoman, "Pacino Wants to Be Fair to Shakespeare," *The New York Times*, October 29, 2010.

213 Anita Singh, "Al Pacino on Directing: I Feel Like a Dilettante," *The Telegraph*, September 5, 2011.

Sidebar Notes

a Andrew Yule, *op. cit.*, p. 5.

b Andrew Yule, *op. cit.*, p. 141.

c Lawrence Grobel, *op. cit.*, p. 28.

d *Cambridge Dictionaries Online*, Cambridge University Press, retrieved October 18, 2012, from http://dictionary.cambridge.org/dictionary/british/method-acting.

e *...And Justice for All* production notes, Columbia Pictures, 1979.

f "What Is Method Acting?," The Lee Strasberg Theatre and Film Institute, retrieved October 18, 2012 from http://www.methodactingstrasberg.com/methodacting.

g *...And Justice for All* production notes.

h Sidney Lumet, *Making Movies*, Alfred A. Knopf, 1995, pp. 120–121.

i *The Godfather Part II* press notes, Paramount Pictures, 1974.

j *...And Justice for All* production notes.

k Andrew Yule, *op. cit.*, p. 162.

l Mel Gussow, "Lee Strasberg of Actors Studio Dead," *The New York Times*, February 18, 1982.

m Lawrence Grobel, *op. cit.*, p. 86.

n Lawrence Grobel, *op. cit.*, xx.

o Lawrence Grobel, *op. cit.*, p. 76.

p Lawrence Grobel, *op. cit.*, p. 52.

q Lawrence Grobel, *op. cit.*, p. 183.

r Excerpt from "*Heat*'s Hot Cup of Coffee" by Devin Gordon, *Newsweek*, August 29, 2008.

Original title: *Al Pacino*
© 2013 Cahiers du cinéma
SARL

Titre original :
Al Pacino © 2013
Cahiers du cinéma SARL

This Edition published
by Phaidon Press Limited
under licence from
Cahiers du cinéma SARL,
65, rue Montmartre,
75002 Paris, France © 2013
Cahiers du cinéma SARL.

Cette Édition est publiée
par Phaidon Press Limited
avec l'autorisation des
Cahiers du cinéma SARL,
65, rue Montmartre,
75002 Paris, France © 2013
Cahiers du cinéma SARL.

Cahiers du cinéma
65, rue Montmartre
75002 Paris

www.cahiersducinema.com

ISBN 978 0 7148 6664 2

A CIP catalogue record
of this book is available from
the British Library.

Series concept designed
by Thomas Mayfried
Designed by Ron Woods

Printed in China

Acknowledgments

This book was researched
in its entirety at the
Margaret Herrick Library
in Los Angeles, and would
not have been possible
without the help of the
staff there. The following
resources were also
invaluable: The American
Cinematheque, the New
Beverly Cinema, Cinefile
Video, Video Journeys
and the Charles E. Young
Research Library at UCLA.
Special thanks to Valérie
Buffet, Amélie Despérier-
Bougdira, Laura Kern,
Céline Moulard and the
staff at Cahiers du cinéma.
Finally, this book and its
author are indebted to
Rian Johnson — for his love,
support, encouragement,
and perhaps above all,
his willingness to watch
Jack and Jill.

Photographic credits

AMPAS/I.V./MPTV/Photomasi: p. 139;
Artists Entertainment Complex/
Warner Bros. Pictures: pp. 70, 71, 76;
BFI/Paramount Pictures: pp. 19 (b), 20–
21, 25 (t), 28 (t), 31, 32 (b); Christophel/
Universal Pictures: pp. 94, 97, 99 (b),
108; © Christopher Anderson/Magnum
Photos: pp. 174–175; Collection
Cahiers du cinéma/Artists Entertainment
Complex/Warner Bros. Pictures:
pp. 62, 68, 69 (b), 72, 77; Collection
Cahiers du cinéma/CiP/Lorimar Film
Entertainement: p. 176 (bl); Collection
Cahiers du cinéma/D. Rabourdin/
The Caddo Company/United Artists:
p. 104; Collection Cahiers du cinéma/
D. Rabourdin/Warner Bros.: p. 46;
Collection Cahiers du cinéma/
D. Rabourdin: p. 41 (t, b); Collection
Cahiers du cinéma/GGR/New Line
Cinema/Zupnik Cinema Group II:
p. 179 (tl); Collection Cahiers du cinéma/
Goldcrest-Viking/Warner Bros.: p. 176
(br); Collection Cahiers du cinéma/
Paramount Pictures: pp. 28 (b), 32 (t);
Collection Cahiers du cinéma/photo:
Frank Connor © 1995 Warner Bros./
Monarchy Ent. V. B. & Regency Ent.
USA: pp. 148 (b), 149, 150–151, 156;
Collection Cahiers du cinéma/Produzioni
De Laurentiis/Paramount Pictures: p. 48;
Collection Cahiers du cinéma/Twentieth
Century Fox Corporation: pp. 10, 169;
Collection Cahiers du cinéma/Universal
Pictures: pp. 107 (t), 110, 112, 113 (t, b),
116, 119, 120 (t, b), 122–123, 124,
125 (t, b), 129 (t), 130–131, 132 (b), 135;
Collection CAT'S/Artists Entertainment
Complex/Warner Bros. Pictures: pp. 74–
75; Collection CAT'S/Columbia Pictures
Corporation: pp. 81, 84–85, 86 (t, b),
87, 88; Collection CAT'S/Paramount
Pictures: pp. 16, 26; Collection CAT'S/
Produzioni De Laurentiis/Paramount
Pictures: p. 59; Collection CAT'S/
Universal Pictures: cover, pp. 118, 129
(b); Collection CAT'S/Warner Bros./
Monarchy Ent. V. B. & Regency Ent.
USA: pp. 146–147; Collection CAT'S/
Warner Bros.: pp. 34, 37, 45; Collection
Christophel/Alcon Entertainment:
p. 179 (tr); Collection Christophel/
Artists Entertainment Complex/Warner
Bros. Pictures: p. 69 (t); Collection
Christophel/photo: Frank Connor ©
1995 Warner Bros./Monarchy Ent. V. B.
& Regency Ent. USA: pp. 148 (t), 157;
Collection Cinémathèque française/
Artists Entertainment Complex/Warner
Bros. Pictures: pp. 66–67; Collection
Cinémathèque française/Produzioni
De Laurentiis/Paramount Pictures: pp. 52,
56 (t), 58 (b); Collection Cinémathèque
française/Universal Pictures: p. 107 (b);
Collection Cinémathèque française/
Warner Bros.: pp. 176 (tr), 38–39;
Columbia Pictures Corporation:
p. 89; Columbia Pictures/Broken Road
Production/Happy Madison Productions:
pp. 160 (t), 163, 164, 171; © Dennis
Stock/Magnum Photos: p. 43 (b); Getty
Images/Artists Entertainment Complex/
Warner Bros. Pictures: p. 73 (b); © Jerry
Schatzberg: p. 40; © Jose R. Lopez/The
New York Time-REA: p. 43 (t); Margaret
Herrick Library/AMPAS/Paramount
Pictures: pp. 19 (t), 24; Margaret Herrick
Library/AMPAS/photo: Myles Aronowitz/
Universal Pictures: p. 138; Margaret
Herrick Library/AMPAS/Universal
Pictures: pp. 96 (t, b), 102–103; McCabe
Eamonn/Camera Press/Gamma: p. 158;
MPTV/PhotoMasi/Artists Entertainment
Complex/Warner Bros. Pictures: p. 65;
NY Daily News via Getty Images:
p. 64; Paramount Pictures: pp. 22, 27;
Photo12/Columbia Pictures/Broken Road
Production/Happy Madison Productions:
pp. 160 (b), 161, 166–167, 168; Photo12/
Mandalay Entertainment: p. 180 (bl);
Photo12/Millenium Films/Emmett/Furla
Films: p. 153; Photo12/Movision: p. 179
(br); Photo12/New Line Cinema/Niccol
Films: p. 179 (bl); Photo12/Paramount
Pictures: p. 25 (b); Photo12/Produzioni
De Laurentiis/Paramount Pictures: pp. 56
(b), 57; Photo12/Universal Pictures:
pp. 15, 105, 114–115, 140–141; Photo12/
Warner Bros./Monarchy Ent. V. B.
& Regency Ent. USA: p. 180 (tr);
Photofest/Artists Entertainment Complex/
Warner Bros. Pictures: p. 73 (t); Photofest/
Columbia Pictures Corporation:
pp. 80, 83, 92; Photofest: pp. 8, 176 (tl);
Photofest/Universal Pictures: pp. 126,
128, 132 (t); Photofest/Warner Bros./
Monarchy Ent. V. B. & Regency Ent.
USA: p. 152; Private collection/Buena
Onda International/Salomé Productions:
p. 180 (br); Private collection/Columbia:
p. 185; Private collection: p. 117 ; Private
collection/Twentieth Century Fox:
p. 180 (tl); Produzioni De Laurentiis/
Paramount Pictures: p. 53; Ron Galella/
WireImage/Getty: pp. 6, 9, 12; Rue des
Archives/Produzioni De Laurentiis/
Paramount Pictures: pp. 54–55; Rue des
Archives/Universal Pictures: p. 99 (t); Rue
des Archives/Warner Bros./Monarchy
Ent. V. B. & Regency Ent. USA: p. 142;
The Kobal Collection/Columbia Pictures
Corporation: pp. 90–91; The Kobal
Collection/Produzioni De Laurentiis/
Paramount Pictures: pp. 50, 51 (t, b),
58 (t); The Kobal Collection/Warner
Bros./Monarchy Ent. V. B. & Regency
Ent. USA: p. 154; Universal Pictures:
pp. 100, 109, 136, 137; Victoria
University Library, Toronto/Columbia
Pictures Corporation: p. 78; Warner
Bros./Monarchy Ent. V. B. & Regency
Ent. USA: pp. 144, 145; Warner Bros.:
p. 36.

All reasonable efforts have been made
to trace the copyright holders of the
photographs used in this book.
We apologize to anyone that we were
unable to reach.

Cover illustration
Al Pacino in Brian De Palma's *Scarface*
(1983).